# Bloomsbury Professional Law Insight

# Cryptocurrency in Matrimonial Finance

# Bloomsbury Professional Law Insight

# Cryptocurrency in Matrimonial Finance


**Dean Armstrong KC, Barrister, The 36 Group**

**Marc Samuels, Barrister, The 36 Group**



Bloomsbury Professional

LONDON • DUBLIN • EDINBURGH • NEW YORK • NEW DELHI • SYDNEY

BLOOMSBURY PROFESSIONAL

Bloomsbury Publishing Plc

50 Bedford Square, London, WC1B 3DP, UK

1385 Broadway, New York, NY 10018, USA

29 Earlsfort Terrace, Dublin 2, Ireland



**British Library Cataloguing-in-Publication Data**

A catalogue record for this book is available from the British Library.

ISBN: PB: 978 1 52652 140 8
ePDF: 978 1 52652 142 2
ePub: 978 1 52652 141 5

Typeset by Compuscript Ltd, Shannon
Printed and bound by CPI Group (UK) Ltd, Croydon, CR0 4YY

MIX
Paper from responsible sources
FSC® C013604

# Acknowledgments

To my son, Freddie, who continues to provide boundless inspiration for all that I do. To my father Paul, my mother Merle, my sister Paula and to my niece and nephew, Anna and Oliver Cooke, two superb lawyers who are destined for great things.

DEAN ARMSTRONG KC

******

To Anthony and Lorraine Samuels, who continue to be my guides in all things, and to the incomparable clerking team at 36 Family.

MARC SAMUELS

# Contents

# Table of Statutes

# Table of Statutory Instruments

# Table of Cases

**F**



**G**



**H**



**I**



**J**



**K**



**L**



**M**

**T**



**U**



**V**



**W**



**X**



**Y**

*Chapter 1*

# Introduction

**1.01** The cyber law world is evolving at pace. Once of the great challenges facing the courts of England and Wales is the question of how to respond to the instantaneous nature of actions and the need for novel remedies in the digital age. Due to the positive attitudes shown by senior members of the judiciary, and the willingness of the courts to grant relief and apply well-recognised labels to these new developments, it is the view of the authors that England and Wales is one of the most advanced jurisdictions in this burgeoning area of law.

Recent years have seen the courts grapple with responses to technological developments in the fields of blockchain and cryptoassets, with judges being required to consider whether, and if so how, there needs to be departure from orthodox norms and long-established legal principles. Some of the matters considered in this book are the subject of debate in other areas of law where cryptocurrency features. Matrimonial finance is but one frontier. This work looks at some of those challenges and considers how traditional approaches and remedies can be adapted to accommodate this unique asset class which is becoming increasingly mainstream in the age of decentralised finance, cryptoassets, and the metaverse. It is no longer realistic to dismiss cryptocurrencies such as Bitcoin as a marginal type of asset and the preserve of specialists. Their growing popularity and increased market share mean that they will soon be as prominent a feature of divorce as pensions or company shares. At the time of writing, the global market cap for cryptocurrencies is US$1.26 trillion and there are over 18,000 cryptocurrencies in existence.

This work aims to serve two purposes. Firstly, for those unfamiliar with cryptoassets and blockchain / distributed ledger technology, to provide a reliable and practical explanation of how these innovations work and their underlying conceptual bases. Secondly, this book will explore how existing legal concepts may come to be applied to cryptocurrency in the context of matrimonial finance. This raises questions which at first blush seem academic – such as whether cryptoassets constitute 'property' – but are also of practical importance. It also invites consideration of how this exciting asset class should be approached in money cases. By way of example, the nature of cryptocurrency means that the approach to disclosure is likely to be different to the approach taken for, say, an undisclosed bank account.

Chapters 2 and 3 of this book introduce cryptocurrency and blockchain technology and provide examples of the latter's application. They also compare the so-called 'traditional' financial system with that of the decentralised financial system facilitated by blockchain. The reader is also introduced to smart contracts and another popular digital asset, the non-fungible token. Chapter 4 provides a deeper dive into the cryptocurrency ecosystem, introducing the unfamiliar to the key players in the market and explaining associated terminology (such as 'public and private key', 'wallet', 'exchange', and 'miner'). That part of the work closes with information about the current top 10 cryptocurrencies by market capitalisation.

Chapters 5 and 6 provide summaries of the current regulatory arrangements for cryptocurrency in the United Kingdom, as well as an overview of financial remedies and the distributive principles applied by the Family Court in matrimonial finance cases.

As indicated above, Chapter 7 considers whether cryptocurrency constitutes 'property' for the purposes of the Matrimonial Causes Act 1973 and why this matters, as well as reflecting on whether cryptoassets need to be disclosed on Form E. Chapter 8 draws together many of the threads explored in previous chapters in this work. It looks at some of the practical issues that can arise during matrimonial finance proceedings. These include the challenges of identifying and valuing cryptocurrency as well as matters of disclosure, freezing orders, and preservation of devices. The work closes with an outline of the principles applying to 'self-help' disclosure and associated criminal offences pursuant to the Computer Misuse Act 1990 and the Data Protection Act 2018, along with a summary of HMRC's current guidance on the taxation of cryptoassets for individuals.

While the authors are anecdotally aware of numerous cases where the Family Court has dealt with cryptocurrencies, there is yet to be a Family Court authority on how this type of asset should be dealt with. As such, many of the ideas mooted in this book are drawn from analogies in the commercial litigation sphere. It will be updated in further editions as the jurisprudence develops. We have sought to provide an enlightening overview of this specialist area as well as answers to some of the questions that practitioners will be called upon to answer.

The law stated in this work is current as of June 2022.

*Chapter 2*

# An introduction to cryptocurrency



## A. INTRODUCTION

**2.01** The first part of this work looks at the conceptual basis and general characteristics of cryptocurrencies and their associated technologies. It introduces the key operators in the cryptocurrency landscape and various noteworthy cryptocurrencies that are, at present, commanding attention in this rapidly evolving marketplace. This chapter also considers the legal status of cryptocurrencies and related technologies in England and Wales. The regulation of cryptocurrencies in this jurisdiction is addressed in Chapter 5. The chapter closes with a brief history of the most well-known digital currency, Bitcoin.

## B. TYPES OF CRYPTOASSETS

**2.02** A cryptocurrency is a type of cryptoasset, which in turn is but one application of distributed ledger technology ('DLT'). DLT is typically associated with blockchain and ledgers, while cryptocurrency tends to be recorded on those lodgers (as to which, see Chapter 3).

All cryptoassets use and are based on some form of DLT, and the current prevalent cryptoassets are issued using permissionless ledgers.

There are primarily two types of blockchains: private and public blockchains, however these are subject to sub-categories such as 'hybrid' blockchains. A public blockchain (such as the blockchains that support Bitcoin and Litecoin) is a non-restrictive, permissionless distributed ledger system. This means that anybody who has access to the internet can access the blockchain platform and participate in the blockchain network as an authorised node. By contrast, a private blockchain is a restrictive or permissionless blockchain that operates on a closed, usually smaller network. These are typically used in specific enterprises or organisations and participants in the blockchain network are selected. Access, authorisations, permissions, and security is controlled by the organisation running the private blockchain.

Policy and legislative thinking in relation to cryptocurrency and the application of blockchain technology is still very much in its formative years in the UK. The UK government's first expression of policy thinking was set out by the UK Cryptoassets Taskforce in its Final Report, which was published in October 2018 (the '2018 Report')[1] (and which has subsequently been developed by the various Taskforce authorities, HM Treasury, the Bank of England, and the UK Financial Conduct Authority). The 2018 Report explored some of the underlying concepts at play. It acknowledges that while all cryptoassets use some form of DLT, not all applications of DLT involve cryptoassets. Nor is there a single universally applied definition of a 'cryptoasset'. Generally speaking, a cryptoasset is

> 'a cryptographically secured digital representation of value or contractual rights that uses some form of DLT and can be transferred, stored or traded electronically. Examples of cryptoassets include Bitcoin and Litecoin (and other "cryptocurrencies"), and those issued through the Initial Coin Offering (ICO) process, often referred to as "tokens".'[2]

Observing that this is an evolving marketplace where new cryptocurrencies continue to launch at pace (as of January 2022, there are more than 9,000 cryptocurrencies recognised on coinmarketcap.com), the UK Cryptoassets Taskforce categorised cryptoassets as falling into one of three categories:

i. **Exchange tokens**

   This term is often used synonymously with 'cryptocurrencies' (like Bitcoin, Ethereum, Litecoin etc). Exchange tokens use a DLT-derived platform and are decentralised (ie they are not issued by a central bank or financial institution). They can be used as a means of exchange or for investment and do not confer on the owner any of the types of rights or assets that are provided by security tokens or bestow preferential benefits or uses unlike utility tokens (see below). Exchange tokens are typically acquired and used with the intention of providing a means of exchange for goods or services and are used as an alternative to fiat currency if that facility is available. They are also used to facilitate regulated payment services. Cryptocurrencies – the paradigm exchange token – do not give rise to claims on their issuer.

---

1 Cryptoassets Taskforce: Final Report (26 October 2018). https://assets.publishing.service.gov.uk/government/uploads/system/uploads/attachment_data/file/752070/cryptoassets_taskforce_final_report_final_web.pdf.

2 Ibid, at 2.10.

ii. **Security tokens**

Security tokens may provide rights such as ownership, repayment of a precise sum of money (as in the traditional sense of 'security'), or entitlement to a share in future profits. They may also be transferable securities or financial investments under the EU's Markets in Financial Instruments Directive II ('MiFID II'). Security tokens are commonly used for the purposes of direct and indirect investment, as well as a capital raising tool. Security tokens constitute a 'specified investment' for the purposes of the Financial Services and Markets Act 2000 (Regulated Activities) Order.

iii. **Utility tokens**

Utility tokens are a variety of tokens that are intended to provide access digitally to a particular product or service by means of a blockchain-derived infrastructure (eg a DLT platform).

These classifications have been adopted by bodies including the UK Financial Conduct Authority in the context of regulation (see Chapter 5). There are other forms of cryptoassets, most notably non-fungible tokens which are considered in Chapter 3.

For the present purposes, the initial takeaway is that cryptoassets may vary significantly in terms of the rights that they confer upon those holding them, as well as their potential and actual applications.[3] They may also engage specific legislation and/or regulation depending on the type of cryptoasset concerned.

The UK Cryptoassets Taskforce simplified these applications into three core purposes in the 2018 Report. Cryptoassets represent: (i) *a means of exchange*; (ii) *a means of investment* (with both firms and consumers gaining direct and indirect exposure by amassing and/or trading cryptoasset holdings or more traditional financial products referenced to cryptoassets); and (iii) *a means of raising capital* and/or *the creation of decentralised networks* through the process of initial coin offerings ('ICO').

The second takeaway is that 'exchange token' is a term that is used synonymously with 'cryptocurrency'. The former is a subset of 'cryptoasset' according to the UK government.

## C. WHAT IS CRYPTOCURRENCY?

**2.03** Is it possible to define the term 'cryptocurrency'? It was noted in the Law Society's guidance report of January 2022 (prepared in collaboration with Tech London Advocates) that

---

3 Ibid, at 2.10.

one of the main challenges touching upon the connected areas of digital assets, smart contracts, DLT etc is the limitations of universal terminology.[4] The report notes, with embellishment, that there are 'almost as many definitions of a cryptocurrency as there are cryptocurrencies'. It quotes the 2018 Report which acknowledges this issue:

> 'Because of the great variety of systems in use and kinds of assets represented (ranging from purely notional payment tokens such as bitcoins to real-world tangible objects) it is difficult to formulate a precise definition of a cryptoasset and, given the rapid development of the technology, that would not be a useful exercise ... As with cryptoassets, it is difficult, and unlikely to be useful, to try to formulate a precise definition of smart contracts and so we have again sought instead to identify what it is about them that may be legally novel or distinctive.'[5]

Meanwhile, the Bank of England definition is of rather limited assistance:

> 'Well, let's start by breaking down the word "cryptocurrency". The first part of the word, "crypto", means "hidden" or "secret" reflecting the secure technology used to record who owns what, and for making payments between users. The second part of the word, "currency", tells us the reason cryptocurrencies were designed in the first place: a type of electronic cash.'[6]

Authoritative if historic guidance from the European Parliament in July 2018 observed that there is no generally accepted definition of the term 'cryptocurrency' in the regulatory space, and that most international policy makers have refrained from defining the term altogether.[7] As suggested in the 2018 Report, this is in part driven by the fact that this term refers to an array of technological developments that employ cryptography. How cryptocurrencies use cryptography is discussed in Chapter 3.

The European Parliament's *Cryptocurrencies and Blockchain Report* of July 2018, summarising the then-position of the various policy makers (ECB, IMF, BIS, EBA, ESMA, World Bank and FATF) following the emergence of Bitcoin in 2009, offered a workable composite definition:

> 'If we try to summarize all the above definitions, a good summary could be that a cryptocurrency is "a digital representation of value that (i) is intended to constitute a peer-to-peer ("P2P") alternative to government-issued legal tender, (ii) is used as a general-purpose medium of exchange (independent of any central bank), (iii) is secured by a mechanism known as cryptography and (iv) can be converted into legal tender and vice versa".'[8]

The report notes that the term 'cryptocurrency' is in practice often erroneously used in a very broad sense and should be distinguished from cryptographic tokens (which offer a functionality

---

4 The Law Society: Tech London Advocates: Blockchain: Legal and Regulatory Guidance (Second Edition) January 2022, p 166.

5 Cryptoassets Taskforce: Final Report (26 October 2018). https://assets.publishing.service.gov.uk/government/uploads/system/uploads/attachment_data/file/752070/cryptoassets_taskforce_final_report_final_web.pdf.

6 https://www.bankofengland.co.uk/knowledgebank/what-are-cryptocurrencies.

7 '*Cryptocurrencies and Blockchain Report*' of the European Parliament, Policy Department for Economic, Scientific and Quality of Life Policies (Prof. Dr. Robby Houben, Alexander Snyers), PE 619.024 July 2018, at p 23.

8 Ibid.

other than and beyond that of a general-purpose medium of exchange) and cryptosecurities (shares and corporate securities which have employed DLT for their registration, issuance, and transfer).

In this work we also distinguish the classic form of cryptocurrency from those issued by central banks, a development that many governments are exploring at pace. For example, the UK government has been exploring the feasibility and logistics of 'Britcoin' since 2021.[9]

The Law Commission published a call for evidence on digital assets on 30 April 2021, the primary function of which was to seek views about, and evidence of, the ways in which digital assets are being used, treated, and dealt with by market participants. It also sought views on the potential consequences of digital assets being 'possessable'.[10] Its interim update was published on 24 November 2021[11] and the digital assets consultation paper is expected in mid-2022.

Breaking this down, the general features of a cryptocurrency are as follows:

i. a cryptocurrency is a digital representation of value;
ii. they are capable of being used as a medium of exchange independent of any central bank;
iii. they represent a peer-to-peer alternative to fiat currency;
iv. they are secured by cryptography; and
v. they can usually be converted into legal tender (and vice versa).

## D. COMPARING TRANSACTION SYSTEMS: 'TRADITIONAL' FINANCE V CRYPTOCURRENCY

**2.04** Reference has been made to the differences between the so-called 'traditional' banking system and the transaction systems that facilitate the operation of cryptocurrencies. If we take the oldest and best-known cryptocurrency, Bitcoin, as an example, both its transaction system and that of the traditional banking system share a central concept: trust. In a 'traditional' system (by which we are contemplating, for example, high street banks, credit card companies etc), reliance is placed on a network to process transactions where financial institutions are either directly or indirectly connected. When a transaction begins from a payor's account (for example, when using a 'chip and pin' debit to purchase a cup of coffee), the process originates from that individual's bank which then initiates a checking process. This process requires the use of intermediaries. In terms of trust, in a traditional banking context, a payee needs to know that when a payor transacts, say to purchase the coffee, that he actually has the funds, and that the money will be received by the payee.

9 https://www.reuters.com/business/finance/uk-launches-taskforce-potential-bank-england-digital-currency-sunak-2021-04-19/.
10 https://www.lawcom.gov.uk/project/digital-assets/.
11 The interim update is available at: https://s3-eu-west-2.amazonaws.com/lawcom-prod-storage-11jsxou24uy7q/uploads/2021/11/Digital-Assets-Interim-Update-Paper-FINAL.pdf/.

In a physical cash transaction, the problem is minimised as the receipt of banknotes effects the exchange of value without the need for an intermediary. When using a card payment, the payment has to be processed by both card and banking networks for the purposes of authorisation, clearing, and settlement. It is the use of these institutions – reliance on their standing and reputation – that bolsters trust, while they perform various checks during the transaction process. In terms of authorisation, the identity of the transacting party and availability of funds is confirmed. In the clearing phase of the process, information relating to the transaction is communicated and used for the verification of money to be debited from the payor's account (and credited to the payee's account). The final stage in the process is settlement, which occurs daily on an aggregated net-basis and involves the actual movement of funds. As described more fully in a 2019 market insight produced by Wisdom Tree:[12]

> 'The card network computes the net settlement position that the customer's bank needs to pay to the merchant's bank and sends that information to both banks, plus a new actor, the settlement bank. The settlement bank pays the merchant's bank, and the customer's bank pays the settlement bank. Finally, the merchant gets credited, and the customer gets debited. This entire process (authorisation to settlement) generally takes between 24 and 48 hours. [...] it's quite a cumbersome, informationally heavy process and it involves a number of counterparties that need to sequentially create and transmit information. Yet this system is well established and reliable enough that it has built up a high level of trust among users. Indeed, it has become so widely accepted that countries such as Sweden are aiming to become cashless societies.
>
> In this model, the card network plays an essential role. As a lot of actors are involved, all with their own information systems, so it can be quite difficult to communicate between one another. The network "is responsible for collecting all transactions and operating a gateway. It exchanges information between [customers' bank'] and [merchants' banks], establishes rules and processes for participation in the network, creates formatting standards for information going across the network, and facilitates monetary settlement between and among its client banks".[13] In other words, it provides the standards and infrastructure for information exchange between the parties involved.'

How then does the Bitcoin transaction system work and how is 'trust' maintained?

The answer is summarised by Satoshi Nakamoto's (allegedly the founder of Bitcoin) original white paper which in its introduction highlights the perceived shortcomings of the traditional finance system and offers an abstract solution.

> 'Commerce on the Internet has come to rely almost exclusively on financial institutions serving as trusted third parties to process electronic payments. While the system works well enough for most transactions, it still suffers from the inherent weaknesses of the trust based model. Completely

---

12 https://www.wisdomtree.eu/en-ie/-/media/eu-media-files/other-documents/research/market-insights/market-insight-bitcoin-vs-traditional-payment.pdf.

13 Herbst-Murphy, Susan (2013). 'Clearing and Settlement of Interbank Card Transactions: A MasterCard Tutorial for Federal Reserve Payments Analysts'.

> non-reversible transactions are not really possible, since financial institutions cannot avoid mediating disputes. The cost of mediation increases transaction costs, limiting the minimum practical transaction size and cutting off the possibility for small casual transactions, and there is a broader cost in the loss of ability to make non-reversible payments for non-reversible services. With the possibility of reversal, the need for trust spreads. Merchants must be wary of their customers, hassling them for more information than they would otherwise need. A certain percentage of fraud is accepted as unavoidable. These costs and payment uncertainties can be avoided in person by using physical currency, but no mechanism exists to make payments over a communications channel without a trusted party.
>
> What is needed is an electronic payment system based on cryptographic proof instead of trust, allowing any two willing parties to transact directly with each other without the need for a trusted third party. Transactions that are computationally impractical to reverse would protect sellers from fraud, and routine escrow mechanisms could easily be implemented to protect buyers. In this paper, we propose a solution to the double-spending problem using a peer-to-peer distributed timestamp server to generate computational proof of the chronological order of transactions. The system is secure as long as honest nodes collectively control more CPU power than any cooperating group of attacker nodes.'[14]

In essence, the software known as 'Bitcoin' uses blockchain technology, along with cryptographic proofs and game theory, to maintain the integrity of its transactional ledger which records across the Bitcoin network. It does this without the need for a third-party intermediary. It is, therefore, decentralised.

In practical terms, the participant sending bitcoin will enter the recipient's Bitcoin (software) address and the quantity of cryptocurrency that is being transferred. This is achieved using the individual's digital 'wallet' interface. The relevant information is then sent to the Bitcoin network using the sender's private key to digitally authorise (sign) the transaction. This stage is necessary because it proves to other network participants that: (i) it is the participant (the sender) who is authorising this transaction; and (ii) that the participant actually has the coin(s) that are the subject of the transaction. A number of nodes on the network will then receive the transaction before it is broadcast to all nodes. This process takes only a few seconds before the entire network has received details of the transaction.

The next stage is known as cryptographic validation. This is where all nodes on the network agree on the state of the blockchain (in this example, the Bitcoin blockchain). Specifically, all nodes will agree on the transactions that have been approved and which are to be appended to the blockchain. This process is accomplished by 'miner' nodes who compete to solve a computationally intensive cryptographic puzzle which is created by the participant effecting the transaction. The first miner to solve the puzzle notifies the network that the problem has been solved. This can be checked by all other nodes on the network. This process which is undertaken by miner nodes

14 The white paper can be found via https://bitcoin.org/bitcoin.pdf.

is known as a 'proof of work'. They have to invest substantial amounts of computing power to resolve these cryptographic problems. When the majority (more than 50%) of the nodes on the network confirm that completion has been achieved (ie acceptance of a 'proof of work'), then the transaction is approved and a new 'block' is added to the blockchain. This is the equivalent of a settlement phase in a traditional finance transaction – it is the point in time that the cryptocurrency changes ownership. A timestamp is added to the new block that is appended to the blockchain.

The effect of this is that once the blockchain is supplemented by a new block, it would require an enormous, though theoretically available, amount of computing power (agreement of more than 50% of nodes on the network) to amend it. As more blocks are added to the blockchain, it becomes exponentially more difficult to amend. Immutability (the creation of a permanent record) is considered a key feature and attraction of blockchain technology.

Once the block containing the transaction is registered on the ledger and timestamped, the recipient participant will see that the transaction has been confirmed and they will be the new owner of the coin(s).

The stages of a Bitcoin transaction are summarised as follows:[15]

> *Stage 1*. Agreement as to the transaction. Jane has 10 bitcoins to start off with. Jane agrees to pay Will 1 bitcoin for a necklace, plus 0.01 bitcoins as a transaction fee.
>
> *Stage 2*. Creation of the transaction message by Jane. This message includes three elements: a reference to the previous transaction through which Jane acquired her 10 bitcoins; the addresses to pay (which include Will's Bitcoin address), and the amounts to pay each one. The message will also contain digital signatures and any further conditions that Jane may elect to place on the payment.
>
> Inputs:
>
> - 10 bitcoins from Jane (the output from the last transaction she participated in).
>
> Outputs:
>
> - 1 bitcoin to Will.
> - 8.99 bitcoins to Jane (being the 'change' from the transaction).
> - 0.01 bitcoins as a transaction fee (transaction fees are defined implicitly by the difference between inputs and explicitly listed outputs for a transaction).
>
> *Stage 3*. Signing. Once Jane has created the message, she will digitally authenticate it to prove that the transaction message was created by the participant who wants to make payment, ie proving that she controls the payer address.

15 Worked example from https://www.bankofengland.co.uk/-/media/boe/files/quarterly-bulletin/2014/innovations-in-payment-technologies-and-the-emergence-of-digital-currencies.pdf.

*Stage 4*. Broadcast of the message to the Bitcoin network.

*Stage 5*. 'Miners' gather details of Jane's transaction and combine it with others into new candidate 'blocks'. Miners compete to solve a cryptographic puzzle (verification in a way that the other nodes accept).

*Stage 6*. Verification. Steve is a bitcoin 'miner' and successfully verifies a block containing Jane's transaction. Steve will therefore receive both a reward in Bitcoin plus the transaction fee from Jane's transaction. Steve will broadcast the result to other nodes on the network and the block will be added to their copies of the blockchain. Will then receives 1 bitcoin and he delivers the necklace to Jane.

The Bitcoin transaction system has far fewer intermediaries than the 'traditional' banking system. The interaction is simple: the participant's wallet engages with the Bitcoin network which is composed of nodes and miners. Any participant node can join or leave the (permissionless) Bitcoin network at will without impacting its functioning. A key advantage is that this transaction system can be accessed and used at any time and theoretically without error. If the correct quantity of coins and the correct destination address are inputted by the participant, the funds will be transferred to the destination. There are no single points of failure, making fraud and errors practically impossible as the network would only be compromised if more than 50% of the nodes were compromised. The computing power that this would require is so enormous that the likelihood of this occurring is more hypothetical than realistic.

As discussed in later chapters, error and risk usually arise in relation to access to a digital wallet which stores private keys (as access to private keys enables a wrongdoer to handle the owner's cryptocurrency). 'Wallets', 'private keys', and other key terminology are explained in Chapter 4.

## E. THE LEGAL STATUS OF CRYPTOCURRENCY IN THE UNITED KINGDOM

**2.05** As suggested above, UK policy thinking in relation to cryptocurrency is developing rapidly. At present there is no specific legislation governing cryptocurrency in the UK. However, due to a number of recent decisions in the courts of England and Wales, it is the authors' view that this jurisdiction currently boasts the most developed jurisprudence in this field.

Although the financial regulators have previously issued warnings in relation to investment in cryptoassets, they are not subject to a ban or blanket prohibition in this jurisdiction.[16] However, some cryptoassets will be subject to financial regulation, and there may also be UK payment services and electronic money regulatory issues, as well as the implications of the UK anti-money

16 See, eg, the consumer page on the FCA website for cryptoassets: https://www.fca.org.uk/consumers/cryptoassets.

laundering regime which now extends to capture activities relating to most cryptoassets irrespective of their being subject to financial regulation.

The key point to note is that cryptoassets (including cryptocurrencies) are not recognised as a legal tender or the equivalent to fiat currency in the UK.

In terms of legal status, an ancillary issue of whether cryptoassets constitute 'property' has been explored by the courts following the UK Jurisdictional Taskforce's *Legal Statement on Cryptoassets and Smart Contacts* in 2019.[17] Despite neither constituting a chose in possession (physical item) nor a chose in action (a right capable of enforcement), the statement observed that a strict interpretation of those categories would be unsuitable and there were compelling reasons why cryptocurrencies should be recognised as property. This matters because:

> '[I]n principle proprietary rights are recognised against the whole world, whereas other – personal – rights are recognised only against someone who has assumed a relevant legal duty. Proprietary rights are of particular importance in an insolvency, where they generally have priority over claims by creditors, and when someone seeks to recover something that has been lost, stolen or unlawfully taken. They are also relevant to the questions of whether there can be a security interest in a cryptoasset and whether a cryptoasset can be held on trust.
>
> The term property is also part of the lexicon of the law: it is widely used in statutes and cases. It is important to understand whether the many statutory and common law rules applicable to property apply also to cryptoassets, and, if so, how. Of particular significance are the rules concerning succession on death, the vesting of property in personal bankruptcy, the rights of liquidators in corporate insolvency, and tracing in cases of fraud, theft or breach of trust. It would, to say the least, be highly unsatisfactory if rules of that kind had no application to cryptoassets.'

There have been many recent cases where interim relief including freezing orders have been made by the courts to preserve cryptoassets, as in *AA v Persons Unknown* where the court specifically endorsed the UKJT legal statement, upholding cryptocurrency's status as property.[18]

Most recently, the judgment of Mrs Justice Falk in *Tulip Trading Limited v Bitcoin Association for BSV & Ors* says the following at [140–141]:

> '140. TTL maintains that the bitcoin held at the 1Feex and 12ib7 addresses constitute property, that the claim relates to that property and that it is located in the jurisdiction. It did not seek to rely on the private keys themselves constituting property.
>
> 141. The Defendants did not take issue in oral submissions with the classification of the bitcoin as property, or that the claim relates to property. Given the Taskforce Statement and the views expressed in cases that have considered the issue (*AA v Persons Unknown* [2019] EWHC 3556 (Comm); [2020]

---

17 A pdf of the report is available at: https://technation.io/lawtech-uk-resources/#cryptoassets.

18 *AA v Persons Unknown* [2019] EWHC 3556.

4 WLR 35 at [61]; *Ion Science Limited & Anor v Persons Unknown* (unreported), 21 December 2020 ("*Ion Science*") at [11]; *Fetch.AI Limited v Persons Unknown* [2021] EWHC 2254 (Comm) ("*Fetch.AI*") at [9] – albeit all in connection with interim relief) I am satisfied that TTL has the better of the arguments on these points.'[19]

This is considered in detail in Chapter 7 in the context of matrimonial finance.

## F. CASE STUDY: THE EVOLUTION OF BITCOIN

**2.06** Bitcoin is the oldest cryptocurrency in circulation, and it remains the most well-known, even though it was preceded by commodity-related virtual currencies introduced in the 1990s.

Bitcoin is usually described as a virtual, decentralised and ostensibly anonymous currency that is neither government-backed or controlled or backed by any other legal entity, and it cannot be exchanged into gold or any other commodity.[20]

As suggested above, Bitcoin's protocol is founded on a 'proof of work' consensus mechanism. The issuance of bitcoins takes place via a process known as 'mining'. This process – the entirety of which is publicly visible and available via open-source software – involves the participants making their computers available to the Bitcoin network to solve complex cryptographic problems. The resolution of these puzzles (and, as a consequence, the creation of 'blocks') results in 'rewards' of bitcoins.

The Bitcoin blockchain is the paradigm example of an open, permissionless blockchain. Any participants can join or leave the network without having to obtain approval from any authority. All that an individual needs to join the Bitcoin network is a computer and the relevant software.

Note that the aggregate number of Bitcoins that can be created through mining is limited:

> 'The Bitcoin system is programmed so that the development of blocks in time will be rewarded with increasingly less Bitcoins and that at no point in time will more than 21 million Bitcoins exist. The fact that the creation and the increase of Bitcoins is automated and limited by the system itself implies that there is no need for the intervention of a central entity / authority to issue Bitcoins.
>
> The limited number of Bitcoins, together with the fact that conversion rates for Bitcoins are determined by supply and demand, without a government body being able to intervene (e.g. by printing additional money), results in a high volatility in Bitcoins prices.'[21]

---

19 *Tulip Trading Ltd v Bitcoin Association For BSV & Ors* [2022] EWHC 667 (Ch).

20 'Cryptocurrencies and Blockchain Report' of the European Parliament, Policy Department for Economic, Scientific and Quality of Life Policies (Prof. Dr. Robby Houben, Alexander Snyers), PE 619.024 July 2018. At 31–32, citing inter alia R Grinberg, 'Bitcoin: An Innovative Alternative Digital Currency' (2011) 4 *Hastings Science & Technology Law Journal* 160.

21 Ibid, citing NM Kaplanov, 'Nerdy Money: Bitcoin, the private digital currency, and the case against its regulation' [2012] *Temple Law Review* 8.

It is often said that that Bitcoin is an anonymous cryptocurrency. This is generally accurate. Although all participants can verify the chain of transactions via the public ledger, there are no immediate means of connecting (identifying) specific Bitcoins to specific individuals. However, it is technically possible, if complex and often costly, to identify the parties behind a Bitcoin transaction by associating various factors that accompany a specific transaction. It is for this reason that the European Parliament has referred to Bitcoin as a 'pseudo-anonymous' coin.

This is a developing area of technology and specialist expertise that will play an increasingly central role in litigation, including in instances of non-disclosure in matrimonial finance proceedings.

At the heart of Bitcoin stands the seminal text referred to above, '*Bitcoin: a Peer-to-Peer Electronic Cash System*' written by Satoshi Nakamoto, which was published online in 2008.[22]

Nakamoto was responsible for creating much of the official Bitcoin software and was active in introducing modifications and posting technical information on the Bitcoin forum.[23] It is not known whether Satoshi Nakamoto is a real person or persons, a pseudonym, or conceivably a number of hackers. After years of speculation, the inventor(s) of this technology remains unknown, and this has lent a popular and compelling mystique to Bitcoin and its operation.

The text itself contained various ideas that integrated with the contemporary thinking in the cryptographic community. It is from this work and the ideas contained in it that Bitcoin evolved rapidly into what it is today, a significant store of value both online and offline.

On 4 January 2008, before the aforementioned paper was posted online on 31 October 2008, the domain name bitcoin.org was registered. On 3 January 2009, the bitcoin network first came into existence with Nakamoto mining the 'genesis block' (block number zero), which had a reward of 50 bitcoins (ie the first 50 bitcoins created). As an assumed timestamp on the coinbase of the block was the text 'The Times 03/Jan/2009 Chancellor on brink of second bailout for banks',[24] a likely satirical inclusion given the instability of the traditional banking system at that time. The 'genesis' block was hardcoded into the Bitcoin software and the 50 bitcoins that were created cannot be spent (as a result of the way that the code was written). The rationale for this is unclear. It is one of the various mysteries stemming from the birth of Bitcoin. The next transaction took place six days after the creation of the genesis block. This is thought by some to be a re-enactment of the creation of the world in the Book of Genesis.

---

22 This text can be found via https://bitcoin.org/bitcoin.pdf.

23 https://en.wikipedia.org/wiki/History_of_bitcoin.

24 Ibid. Davis, J (10 October 2011). 'The Crypto-Currency'. *The New Yorker*. Archived from the original on 23 August 2013.

The first ever Bitcoin transaction took place on 12 January 2009 between Nakamoto and the late Hal Finney, an early collaborator to the project. Nakamoto sent Finney 10 bitcoins. Ten months later, on 5 October 2009, the New Liberty Standard set the first ever Bitcoin exchange rate against the dollar. At the time, US$1 was the equivalent of 2300.03 bitcoins.

In its early days, Bitcoin was predominantly traded and developed by cryptocurrency enthusiasts who transacted between themselves. The first recorded transaction in Bitcoin for physical goods took place when programmer Laszlo Hanyecz purchased two Papa John's pizzas from his fellow crypto enthusiast Jeremy Sturdivant, for 10,000 Bitcoins.[25] The nominal value of a single bitcoin at that time was approximately US$0.004. At the time of writing, those 10,000 bitcoins are today worth approximately US$425 million.

Over the course of 2011–2012, Bitcoin trading gained its footing, with the earliest major transactions occurring on the black markets, the most notorious being the online drug trafficking syndicate, Silk Road. Participants in the syndicate had been paying for drugs with Bitcoin so as to preserve anonymity. Shortly before the fifth anniversary of the Bitcoin white paper, the dark website was shut down and over 26,000 bitcoins were seized (the price of Bitcoin dropped from US$139 to US$109 in a matter of hours). This development shone light both on the apparent criminal activity and the cryptocurrency itself.

Thereafter, Bitcoin trading continued to increase, but not without highs and lows.

In November 2013, a single bitcoin was worth the equivalent of an ounce of gold (approximately US$1,000), though this was short-lived as it plummeted to US$600 the following month. The years that followed saw signs of mainstream adoption, such as in December 2014 when Microsoft began accepting payments in Bitcoin. This was a noteworthy milestone and a sign of early approval and adoption by global businesses.[26] As noted in Gareth Jenkinson's article in 2018 for cointelegraph.com, another milestone was reached when the cryptocurrency appeared on the front page of *The Economist* on 31 October 2015, some six years after Nakamoto released the seminal white paper.

Bitcoin's largest bull run began in 2017, which proved to be its year of prolific growth. Having reached US$1,000 in 2014, it again hit this peak on 2 January 2017. By 11 June 2017, it crossed the US$3,000 threshold and US$5,000 on 2 September 2017. The cryptocurrency continued to gain value, buoyed by the assumption that the launch of Bitcoin futures at the end of the year would draw-in institutional money into the cryptocurrency. During that year it hit a high of US$20,000 before slumping to US$13,000 by 31 December 2017. This period saw an explosion

---

25 https://cointelegraph.com/news/a-brief-history-of-bitcoin-10-years-of-highs-and-lows.

26 Ibid.

of entrepreneurial activity in London and Silicon Valley where multiple market participants and institutional players made moves to capitalise on the potential afforded by Bitcoin and DLT generally.

In the years that followed, Bitcoin has continued to attract widespread media attention. Its colossal highs tempered by characteristic and frequently extreme volatility has surrounded cryptocurrency with a miasma of excitement which has drawn in enormous numbers of investors.

At the time of writing, Bitcoin is trading at US$42,627.00 (GBP £31,155.80). This seismic growth has also brought cryptocurrencies to the fore in terms of legislative thinking, both from a regulatory and tax perspective.

The regulation of Bitcoin and other cryptocurrencies in the UK are considered in Chapter 5.

The key events in Bitcoin's history[27] are summarised in the following timeline:

| **Date** | **Event** |
|---|---|
| **2008** | |
| **4 Jan 2008** | bitcoin.org domain name is registered. |
| **31 Oct 2008** | Satoshi Nakamoto's white paper titled *Bitcoin: A Peer-to-Peer Electronic Cash System* is posted online to a cryptography mailing list. |
| **2009** | |
| **3 Jan 2009** | The Bitcoin network is created with Satoshi Nakamoto mining the genesis block. |
| **9 Jan 2009** | The first open source Bitcoin client was released. |
| **12 Jan 2009** | The first bitcoin transaction between Hal Finney and Satoshi Nakamoto. |
| **5 Oct 2009** | The first bitcoin exchange rate against the dollar: US$1 = 2,300 bitcoins. |
| **2010** | |
| **22 May 2010** | The first transaction where 10,000 mined bitcoins were exchanged for two pizzas. |
| **12 July 2010** | Bitcoin's price increases by 1000%: US$0.008 to US$0.08. |
| **2011** | Based on bitcoin's open-source code, other cryptocurrencies started to emerge. |
| **Jan 2011** | The Electronic Frontier Foundation, a non-profit group, started accepting bitcoins in January 2011 before ceasing to accept them in June 2011, citing concerns about a lack of legal precedent about new currency systems. The decision was reversed on 17 May 2013. |
| **28 Jan 2011** | 25% of all Bitcoin coins are already mined. |
| **9 Feb 2011** | Bitcoin reaches parity with US$. |
| **June 2011** | Bitcoin reaches parity with US$. |
| **8 June 2011** | Bitcoin rises to US$31.91. |
| **12 June 2011** | Bitcoin dips to US$10.25 (known as the 'great bubble'). |

*(continued)*

27 https://en.wikipedia.org/wiki/History_of_bitcoin.

***(Continued)***

| Date | Event |
|---|---|
| **2012** | |
| **Sept 2012** | The Bitcoin Foundation is launched to 'accelerate the global growth of bitcoin through standardization, protection, and promotion of the open source protocol'. |
| **Oct 2012** | BitPay reports having over 1,000 merchants accepting bitcoin under its payment processing service. |
| **28 Nov 2012** | Bitcoin rewards for mining are halved from 50 to 25 coins per block. |
| **2013** | |
| **Feb 2013** | Coinbase reports selling US$1 million worth of bitcoins in a single month at over US$22 per bitcoin. |
| **March 2013** | The US Financial Crimes Enforcement Network (FinCEN) established regulatory guidelines for 'decentralized virtual currencies' such as bitcoin, classifying American bitcoin miners who sell their generated bitcoins as Money Service Businesses (or MSBs), that may be subject to registration and other legal obligations. |
| **9 April 2013** | Bitcoin rises above US$200. |
| **15 May 2013** | US authorities seize accounts associated with Mt. Gox after discovering that it had not registered as a money transmitter with FinCEN in the US. |
| **23 June 2013** | The US Drug Enforcement Administration listed 11.02 bitcoins as a seized asset in a United States Department of Justice seizure notice pursuant to 21 U.S.C. § 881. This marked the first time a government agency claimed to have seized bitcoin. |
| **Oct 2013** | The FBI seized roughly 26,000 bitcoins from website Silk Road. |
| **2014** | |
| **16 April 2014** | Mt. Gox liquidation begins. |
| **Sept 2014** | TeraExchange, LLC, receives approval from the US Commodity Futures Trading Commission to begin listing an over-the-counter swap product based on the price of a bitcoin. The CFTC swap product approval marks the first time a US regulatory agency approved a bitcoin financial product. |
| **11 Dec 2014** | Microsoft begins to accept bitcoin to buy Xbox games and Windows software. |
| **13 March 2014** | Warren Buffett described bitcoin as a 'mirage'. |
| **2015** | |
| **Jan 2015** | Coinbase raises US$75 million as part of a Series C funding round, smashing the previous record for a bitcoin company. |
| **Feb 2015** | The number of merchants accepting bitcoin exceeded 100,000. |
| **31 Oct 2015** | Bitcoin appears on the front of The Economist. |
| **2016** | |
| **Jan 2016** | The network rate exceeds 1 exahash/sec. |
| **9 July 2016** | Bitcoin mining rewards are reduced to 12.5 coins. |
| **Aug 2016** | Bitfinex is hacked and nearly 120,000 bitcoins (approximately US$60 million) was stolen. |

*(continued)*

***(Continued)***

| Date | Event |
|---|---|
| **2017** | The number of businesses accepting bitcoin continued to increase.<br>Japan passes a law to accept bitcoin as a legal payment method. Russia announces that it will legalise the use of cryptocurrencies such as bitcoin. |
| **2 Jan 2017** | Bitcoin reaches US$1,000. |
| **11 June 2017** | Bitcoin reaches US$3,000. |
| **1 Aug 2017** | Bitcoin splits into two derivative digital currencies, the bitcoin (BTC) chain with 1 MB blocksize limit and the Bitcoin Cash (BCH) chain with 8 MB blocksize limit. The split has been called the Bitcoin Cash 'hard fork'. |
| **2 Sept 2017** | Bitcoin reaches US$5,000. |
| **29 Nov 2017** | Bitcoin reaches US$11,000. |
| **17 Dec 2017** | Bitcoin reaches US$20,000 (followed by volatility, leading to approximately US$13,000 by 31 December 2017). |
| **2018** | |
| **22 Jan 2018** | South Korea introduces regulations requiring all the bitcoin traders to reveal their identity. |
| **25 Jan 2018** | George Soros referred to bitcoin as a 'bubble"' |
| **16 March 2018** | Bitcoin hits lowest point in 2018 at US$5,000. |
| **2020** | |
| **27 July 2020** | Bitcoin trading at US$10,944 (recovered value lost in Covid-19-related crash). |
| **3 Sept 2020** | The Frankfurt Stock Exchange admitted in its Regulated Market the quotation of the first bitcoin exchange-traded note. |
| **Oct 2020** | PayPal announces that it would allow its users to buy and sell bitcoin on its platform. |
| **30 Oct 2020** | Bitcoin reaches new all-time high of US$19,850.11. |
| **2021** | |
| **Feb 2021** | The Swiss canton of Zug allows for tax payments in bitcoin and other cryptocurrencies |
| **8 Feb 2021** | Price surge to US$44,200 after Elon Musk and Tesla announcements of investments into Bitcoin and acceptance of Bitcoin for payment. |
| **14 Apr 2021** | Bitcoin reaches all-time high of US$64,800. |
| **19 May 2021** | Bitcoin price drops to US$30,000 following suggestions that Tesla has sold or will sell its Bitcoin holdings. A new set of regulations are announced by the Chinese government relating to cryptocurrency. |
| **20 Oct 2021** | Bitcoin price reaches US$66,974.77. |
| **Dec 2021** | 90% of the total Bitcoin supply of 21 million has been mined according to data from Blockchain.com |
| **2022** | |
| **2 Jan 2022** | Bitcoin hashrate hits an all-time high of 203.5 exahashes per second, Decrypt reports with data from BitInfoCharts. |
| **25 March 2022** | Pavel Zavalny stated that Russia might accept bitcoin for payment for oil and gas exports, in response to sanctions stemming from the 2022 Russian invasion of Ukraine. |
| **27 April 2022** | Central African Republic adopted bitcoin as legal tender alongside the CFA franc. |
| **30 April 2022** | Goldman Sachs gives Bitcoin a further boost by announcing that it had extended a secured lending facility where fiat lending was collateralised on Bitcoin. |

*Chapter 3*

# Blockchain



## A. INTRODUCTION

**3.01** With the introduction of Bitcoin in 2008, the world was also presented with the revolutionary concept of blockchain, which is the underlying technology that facilitates Bitcoin as well as many other cryptocurrencies that followed. The technology is often described as both revolutionary and evolutionary. Its disruptive capability and numerous potential applications are still being explored. It will be many years before the full potential of blockchain comes to fruition.

As discussed in the previous chapter, the first form of decentralised blockchain technology was envisaged by the person (or group of people) known as Satoshi Nakamoto in 2008. Nakamoto employed a Hashcash-like method to timestamp blocks without requiring them to be signed by a trusted third party. It also introduced a difficulty parameter to stabilise the speed and rate at which blocks are added to the chain.[1] This design was implemented the following year as the core protocol for the cryptocurrency known as Bitcoin. It has since been used to provide a public ledger for the transactions taking place on the network.

Many organisations around the globe are already implementing blockchain technology into their operations. Decentralised finance ('DeFi'), for example, is seen as a ground-breaking means of

1 Narayanan, A; Bonneau, J; Felten, E; Miller, A; Goldfeder, S, *Bitcoin and cryptocurrency technologies: a comprehensive introduction*. (Princeton: Princeton University Press, 2016), cited in https://en.wikipedia.org/wiki/Blockchain.

decentralising the current financial system, allowing participants to have greater control over their assets, applying them and transacting without the use of third party intermediaries. As discussed in the previous chapter, this provides a challenge to the slower 'traditional' financial system which relies on participation by trusted third parties.

First-generation blockchain and DLTs have already demonstrated the feasibility of numerous applications, such as the trading, clearing, and settlement of cryptocurrency. However, many commentators have asserted that these have proved impractical to scale, energy-ravenous, and comparatively slow. Today, maturing technologies, evolving standards, and new delivery models are encouraging adoption. In particular, the financial services industry is driving forward the leveraging of blockchain and other DLT platforms. This has been encouraged by the promise of safer, more efficient transactions. The benefits are equally enticing for organisations that want to access and share data and which require visibility when it comes to transaction history. Deloitte's recent analysis observes:

> 'Typically, this is an expensive, inefficient process lacking trust and security. As the potential emerges for blockchain and other DLTs to bolster the efficiency of business operations and create new ways of delivering value, many forward-thinking companies in other industries are implementing and integrating these technologies into existing infrastructures and road maps.
>
> In fact, the vast majority of participants in Deloitte's 2021 Global Blockchain Survey (80%) say their industries will see new revenue streams from blockchain, digital assets, and/or cryptocurrency solutions. And global spending is soaring, with one research firm predicting that it should increase from US$5.3 billion in 2021 to US$34 billion in 2026. According to another analysis, banking leads in blockchain adoption, followed by telecommunications, media, and entertainment; manufacturing; health care and life sciences; retail and consumer goods; and government. Retail and consumer goods are projected to see the fastest growth in blockchain spending between now and 2024.'[2]

In its analysis, Deloitte identifies the following use cases as gaining particular traction:

- *Self-sovereign data and digital personal identity*. This involves leveraging blockchain and other DLT platforms for secure data storage and management, allowing users to create and control tamper-proof digital identities. This has the potential to enhance the security of personally identifiable information and obstruct counterfeiting and cases of stolen identities. Applications include contact-tracing, electronic health records and credentials, and electronic voting.
- *Data sharing between third parties*. Private and permissionless DLT platforms can facilitate secure interaction between organisations, the imperative being to restrict access to specific data only to trusted parties. The technology can allow data to cross corporate and industry boundaries, with information being transferred securely between parties.

---

2 https://www2.deloitte.com/us/en/insights/focus/tech-trends/2022/blockchain-trends.html.
A copy of the report is available at: https://www2.deloitte.com/us/en/insights/topics/understanding-blockchain-potential/global-blockchain-survey.html.

- *Grant funding*, particularly in the context of monitoring and reporting financial and performance results.
- *Intercompany accounting*, as well as *clearance and settlement*, can be time- and resource-intensive for large organisations operating via multiple legal entities. Blockchain and other DLT platforms can improve traceability, transparency, and auditability of inter-entity transfers accounting. This may be particularly useful in a mergers and acquisitions context.
- *Supply chain transparency*. The technology can be used to optimise product-tracking and traceability and obstruct the trading of counterfeit products and illegal or sub-standard components and ingredients. It could also assist governments in enforcing trade policies and to enforce tariffs. On a practical front, it can be used to track assets and shipments, allowing for greater transparency during the procurement process.
- *Customer and audience engagement*. Selling non-fungible tokens is an increasingly popular way for notable people, businesses, and brands to generate digital communities and engage with customers and fan bases (as to which, see further below).
- *Creator monetisation*. Blockchain and other DLT platforms allows content creators to embed their intellectual property with a smart contract that is executed every time the intellectual property is downloaded. That contract can trigger automatic payment based on user identity.

Deloitte's analysis, following the 2021 Global Blockchain Survey,[3] underpins several findings that illustrate a seismic shift in financial services – the sector that is very much leading the way in this field – resulting from the evolution of blockchain and blockchain-based digital assets. Further potential applications of blockchain are discussed below.

## B. WHAT IS BLOCKCHAIN?

**3.02** It is important to maintain a clear distinction between blockchain and cryptocurrency.

Cryptocurrency, for the most part, requires blockchain technology to provide the immutable record of transactions. However, blockchain, and other decentralised ledger technology ('DLT') can, and increasingly does, exist and have functionality outside of cryptocurrency. Blockchain is a type of DLT. DLT is technology that facilitates the recording and sharing of data across multiple data stores (ledgers), where each have identical data records and are collectively maintained and controlled by a distributed network of computer servers (known as 'nodes').

Blockchain uses a method of encryption known as cryptography and employs mathematical algorithms to create and verify a continuously growing data structure.

---

3 Ibid.

Data can only be added to this structure. Existing data cannot be removed. This takes the form of a chain of 'blocks', which functions as a distributed ledger.[4]

A technical definition for blockchain could be as follows: *a peer-to-peer, distributed ledger that is cryptographically secure, append-only, immutable, and updatable only via consensus*.[5]

Breaking that definition down, 'peer-to-peer' means that there is no central authority controlling the network. It is 'decentralised'. All nodes participating in the network communicate with each other directly, allowing the transaction to be effected without third-party intermediaries. As indicated above, a distributed ledger is the central construct of DLT. It means that there is a ledger that is shared and accessed in identical form by all participants on the network.

The reference to 'cryptographic security' refers to the use of cryptography as a means of protecting the distributed ledger from improper use or tampering, as well as maintaining data authentication and integrity. Another hallmark of blockchain is that it is append-only as well as immutable. The former refers to the fact that data is added (in blocks) to the blockchain in a strict time-stipulated sequence. The effect of this is that once data is added, it is almost impossible to amend the blockchain without the consensus of the majority of nodes on the network (theoretically possible but likely impracticable). The result is that to all intents and purposes, data cannot be removed once added. It is immutable.

The final element of the definition looks to the only way that a blockchain can be amended: by consensus. This feature allows the technology to operate without a centralised authority. No one person or body amends the ledger. Rather, the blockchain is only updated when consensus has been reached among those participating on the network. 'To achieve consensus, there are various consensus facilitation algorithms that ensure all parties agree on the final state of the data on the blockchain network and resolutely agree upon it to be true.'[6]

As suggested above, blockchain and related technologies are in their nascent years. A particular application of blockchain technology can have various features, including whether it is fully 'permissionless' or not. On an open, permissionless blockchain, any participant can join or leave the network as they wish. No authorisation is needed from any authority – all they need is the correct software on their computer. In an open, permissionless blockchain, identical copies of the ledger are distributed to every participant in the network. This type of blockchain is utilised for many of the major cryptocurrencies in circulation, including Bitcoin, Ether, Litecoin etc).

---

4 'Cryptocurrencies and Blockchain Report' of the European Parliament, Policy Department for Economic, Scientific and Quality of Life Policies (Prof. Dr. Robby Houben, Alexander Snyers), PE 619.024 July 2018, at p 15.

5 Bashir, I, *Mastering Blockchain*, 3rd edn (Packt Publishing, 2020) 12.

6 Ibid 13.

By contrast, in a 'permissioned' blockchain, network administrators will provide authorisation for a node to join a network, which has the effect of allowing those nodes to be easily identified and monitored. Trust is bestowed on the network administrators who admit or deny access to participants. In an open permissioned blockchain, transactions can be effected and validated without third party intermediaries. Examples of cryptocurrencies that use public permissioned blockchains include Ripple and NEO.[7]

A common question is what is the difference between blockchain and DLT? In essence, and though they are sometimes used interchangeably, blockchain is a form of DLT.

Although they share many characteristics (such as decentralisation, the use of recorded ledgers, and transparency), blockchain is a type of DLT that has gained prominence given the growth of cryptocurrencies. Blockchain is a specific way of structuring data on a DLT platform.

There is no standard form of DLT. The specific combination of features will depend on what a particular DLT platform is being used for and the design choices made by the platform developers. Having said that, DLT platforms usually combine aspects of the following common features:

1. *Data distribution*. Participants all retain a copy of the ledger and have constant access to the data contained on it.
2. *Decentralisation*. Participants are permitted to update the ledger, subject to the degree of control and processes that are subscribed to.
3. *Application of cryptography*. Cryptography can be applied to identify and authorise participants when approval is required. It can also facilitate consensus and confirm data records.
4. *Programmability/automation*. Computer-coded automation, such as smart contracts (as to which, see below) can automatically implement the terms of an agreement, such as automatically triggering interest payments on a bond.[8]

## C. HOW BLOCKCHAIN WORKS

**3.03** A blockchain is a type of distributed database, a ledger that all nodes on the network can see. Nodes are either block signers who validate transactions or they are miners who create new

7 'Cryptocurrencies and Blockchain Report' of the European Parliament, Policy Department for Economic, Scientific and Quality of Life Policies (Prof. Dr. Robby Houben, Alexander Snyers), PE 619.024 July 2018, at p 16, citing inter alia World Bank Group (Natarajan, H; Krause, S and Gradstein, H), 'Distributed Ledger Technology (DLT) and blockchain', 2017, FinTech note, no. 1. Washington, D.C., and Witzig, P and Salomon, V, 'Cutting out the middleman: a case study of blockchain-induced reconfigurations in the Swiss Financial Services Industry', Working Paper 1, 2018/E, the Circulation of Wealth, Université de Neuchâtel.

8 Cryptoassets Taskforce: Final Report (26 October 2018), at 2.3. https://assets.publishing.service.gov.uk/government/uploads/system/uploads/attachment_data/file/752070/cryptoassets_taskforce_final_report_final_web.pdf.

blocks and mint coins. The process by which transactions are validated on the blockchain and how blocks are added can be summarised in the following stages.

| | |
|---|---|
| 1. | **A node starts a transaction.**<br>The participant inputs the relevant information about the transaction and digitally signs it with their private key. 'Transactions' can take various forms and can involve two or more parties. In the context of cryptocurrency, it is a transfer of value. |
| 2. | **The transaction is validated and broadcast.**<br>The transaction is broadcasted to every party on the network in an encrypted form. The fact of the transaction is announced but the details of it are not made public. The other network nodes collectively determine the transaction's validity in accordance with an algorithmic validation method known as the 'consensus mechanism'. |
| 3. | **A new block is identified.**<br>Miner nodes receive the transaction and validate it before adding it to a block. At this stage the process of 'mining' begins whereby miner nodes race to complete the block that they have created. Once a specific miner completes a complex mathematical puzzle, the block they are finalising is considered 'found'. This confirms the completion of the transaction. In many cases, completion of these puzzles provides a reward to the successful miner in the form of coins plus a transaction fee. The quantity of coins provided to the miner depends on the specific cryptocurrency. For bitcoin it is currently 6.25 bitcoins as a reward. The reward amount is cut in half approximately every four years, or every 210,000 blocks. As of April 2022, bitcoin traded at around US$40,000, making 6.25 bitcoins worth nearly US$250,000. |
| 4. | **The new block is added to the blockchain.**<br>The newly created block is validated and the transaction (say, the transfer of cryptocurrency from party A to party B) is completed, and it is broadcast to other participants in the network. The participants then validate and execute the block, which becomes a part of the blockchain. The next block that follows then connects to this block by a link called a hash-pointer.[9] |

## D. THE CONSENSUS MECHANISM

**3.04** From one perspective, a blockchain consists of several layers:[10]

- Infrastructure (hardware).
- Networking (node discovery, information propagation (broadcasting), and verification).
- Consensus.
- Data (blocks, transactions).
- Application (eg smart contracts, decentralised applications).

Of these layers, the consensus mechanism allows transactions to be validated without centralised control. It is a cryptographic means of validation that guarantees the correct sequencing of

---

9 Bashir, I, *Mastering Blockchain*, 3rd edn (Packt Publishing, 2020) 20–21.

10 Chen, H; Pendleton, M; Njilla, L; Xu, S (12 June 2020). 'A Survey on Ethereum Systems Security: Vulnerabilities, Attacks, and Defenses'.

transactions on the blockchain. In practical terms, a consensus mechanism is simply a process that must be undertaken by most or all nodes on a blockchain whereby they agree on a proposed state or value. The reason that sequencing is important is because of the problem of 'double-spending', ie the possibility that the same asset could be transferred more than once given that transfers are neither registered nor controlled centrally. In other words, without a safeguard, an individual could 'spend' money that has already been spent simply because there is no centralised authority (such as a bank) authorising all transactions.

There are different types of consensus mechanisms. The mechanism of choice will be determined by the blockchain itself.

At present, the most common are the Proof of Work ('PoW') mechanism and the Proof of Stake ('PoS') mechanism.

The PoW mechanism is a type of cryptographic proof in which the 'prover' proves to other participants (the 'verifiers') that adequate computational effort has been expended. Verifiers subsequently confirm this expenditure with minimal effort on their part. Central to PoW schemes are their asymmetry: the 'work' (the computation) must place a burden of a certain degree of difficulty on the prover while also being sufficiently easy to check for the verifiers. This concept is known as a CPU cost function, client puzzle, or computational puzzle. A common feature of PoW mechanisms are incentives whereby expenditure of computational capacity is rewarded with value (eg rewards in cryptocurrency). The rewards encourage provers to maintain the network. The purpose of PoW mechanisms is not to prove that certain work has been carried out or that the computational puzzle is 'solved', but rather to deter manipulation of data by establishing large energy expenditure and hardware-control requirements to be able to do. It is also prohibitively expensive for any one party to hijack the network.

PoW systems have been criticised because of the environmental implications of such a high degree of energy consumption.[11] In some instances, this can be more energy than is used by entire countries. The largest country for Bitcoin mining is the US, which accounts for 42.7% of Bitcoin mining activities. According to *Investopedia*, approximately 37 kilotons of electronic waste are annually produced as a by-product of Bitcoin mining.[12]

Bitcoin and Ethereum 1.0 are examples of cryptocurrencies that use a PoW consensus mechanism.

---

11 https://en.wikipedia.org/wiki/Proof_of_work, citing Kharif, O (30 November 2021). 'Analysis | Bye-Bye, Miners! How Ethereum's Big Change Will Work'. *The Washington Post*. Bloomberg News.

12 https://www.investopedia.com/tech/whats-environmental-impact-cryptocurrency.

By contrast, a PoS mechanism operates on the basis that a transaction validator (ie a network node) is selected in proportion to the quantity of a person's holdings of the relevant cryptocurrency. The process of validating a transaction is known as 'forging' rather than 'mining'. The mechanism works on the basis that the would-be validator is sufficiently invested in the cryptocurrency to disincentivise any attack on the network. Potential hijackers would need to acquire a large proportion of the tokens on the blockchain in order to mount an attack. The validator receives a transaction fee for their validation services (which comes from the transacting parties).

Ethereum 2.0, Cardano, Tezos, and other generally newer cryptocurrencies are powered by PoS algorithms.

## E. ADVANTAGES AND DISADVANTAGES OF BLOCKCHAIN

**3.05** The key benefits of blockchain technology are as follows:

1. *Decentralisation.* This is a central concept that underpins blockchain technology. As described above, a consensus mechanism is adopted whereby nodes agree on the validity of transactions and the state of the blockchain. This replaces the need for any trusted third party or intermediaries (such as a financial institution).
2. *Security.* Blockchain offers significant security advantages. All transactions recorded on a blockchain are cryptographically secured. Transactions are verified and only valid transactions are appended to the blockchain. By created a record that cannot be altered and is encrypted end-to-end, blockchain assists in preventing unauthorised activity and wrongdoing. Issues of privacy can also be addressed via blockchain technology by anonymising personal data and imposing permission restrictions on access. Furthermore, information is stored across a network of computers rather than a centralised server. This from one perspective makes it more difficult for hackers to access and hijack data. All actions are secured using private keys and digital signatures (as to which, see Chapter 4).
3. *Transparency.* Because blockchain uses a distributed ledger, all transactions and data stored on it are recorded identically across multiple locations. All participants on the network with access can see the same information at the same time. This allows the system to be fully transparent, which reinforces trust. All transactions are time- and date- stamped and the record is practically immutable, meaning that participants can view the entire history of a transaction. This theoretically eliminates the opportunity for fraud.
4. *Efficiency.* One of the shortcomings of traditional financial systems are that they are often slow, paper-heavy, vulnerable to human error, and usually reliant on third-party involvement. By contrast, blockchain is streamlined. In a financial context, blockchain does not require a protracted process of verification, reconciliation, and clearance. Transactions can therefore be completed faster and there is no need to align multiple ledgers. Documentation can also

be stored on the blockchain along with details of the transaction itself. The system is also readily available as the peer-to-peer nature of the network means that data is replicated and constantly updated across every ledger.

5. *Traceability*. Once data has been appended to the blockchain, it is extremely difficult, if not practically impossible, to amend it. Blockchain therefore creates an immutable audit trail where the history of an asset or transaction is recorded at every juncture. This element of traceability has numerous implications. It can, for example, expose flaws in a product supply chain by recording timings on a product's path to consumer, thereby aiding efficiency.
6. *Automation/facilitation of smart contracts*. Blockchain provides a platform on which transactions can be automated using smart contracts. This can reduce or entirely remove the need for human input. Once prescribed conditions are met, the next stage of a transaction or process is triggered.

These factors do not mean that blockchain is universally lauded and there are some notable and persistent obstructions to the mass adoption of blockchain. For example, while access by participants is relatively straightforward and low-cost, implementation by businesses is usually the opposite. The financial services industry, for example, has seen high implementation costs in these early years of blockchain adoption, and the process is slow-going, often requiring major structural and organisational changes. There are also disadvantages arising out of the intrinsic features of blockchain technology. For example, anonymity is usually perceived as an advantage, safeguarding privacy and control of data. From another perspective anonymity is vulnerable to exploitation and can assist in the concealment of illegal activity or wrongdoing. From a litigation perspective, the identification of wrongdoers or the tracing of undisclosed assets has been an enduring problem associated with cryptocurrency. Separately, the fact that information added to the blockchain is immutable could be problematic where, for example, there has been human error in a transaction or where a smart contract has been poorly drafted. Inviolability can be commercially ruinous in those circumstances. Immutability is also in conflict with recent data protection legislation and regulation, ie, the 'right to be forgotten'.

Noted economists Nouriel Roubini and Preston Byrne have been full-throated when expressing their pessimism:

> 'In reality, blockchain is one of the most overhyped technologies ever. For starters, blockchains are less efficient than existing databases. When someone says they are running something on a blockchain, what they usually mean is that they are running one instance of a software application that is replicated across many other devices.
>
> The required storage space and computational power is substantially greater, and the latency higher, than in the case of a centralised application. Blockchains that incorporate "proof-of-stake" or "zero-knowledge" technologies require that all transactions be verified cryptographically, which slows them down. Blockchains that use "proof-of-work", as many popular cryptocurrencies do, raise yet another

problem: they require a huge amount of raw energy to secure them. This explains why bitcoin "mining" operations in Iceland are on track to consume more energy this year than all Icelandic households combined.

Blockchains can make sense in cases where the speed/verifiability trade-off is actually worth it, but this is rarely how the technology is marketed. Blockchain investment propositions routinely make wild promises to overthrow entire industries, such as cloud computing, without acknowledging the technology's obvious limitations.

Consider the many schemes that rest on the claim that blockchains are a distributed, universal world computer. That claim assumes that banks, which already use efficient systems to process millions of transactions per day, have reason to migrate to a markedly slower and less efficient single cryptocurrency. This contradicts everything we know about the financial industry's use of software. Financial institutions, particularly those engaged in algorithmic trading, need fast and efficient transaction processing. For their purposes, a single globally distributed blockchain such as Ethereum would never be useful.

[...]

Ultimately, blockchain's uses will be limited to specific, well-defined, and complex applications that require transparency and tamper-resistance more than they require speed – for example, communication with self-driving cars or drones. As for most of the coins, they are little different from railway stocks in the 1840s, which went bust when that bubble – like most bubbles – burst.'[13]

## F. APPLICATIONS OF BLOCKCHAIN TECHNOLOGY

**3.06** Though the primary application of blockchain technology was to provide a distributed ledger for cryptocurrencies such as Bitcoin, it has over the years expanded rapidly in its application and is now widely extolled for its ability to transform entire industries. According to PricewaterhouseCoopers, blockchain technology has the potential to generate an annual business value exceeding US$3 trillion by 2030. A study undertaken in 2018 concluded that of 600 business executives surveyed, 84% had at least some exposure to utilising blockchain, indicating an early demand and interest in blockchain technology.[14]

As of 2022, global spending on blockchain technology is forecast to reach nearly US$17.9 billion in 2024, growing at a five-year compound annual growth rate of 46.4%.[15]

The use cases of blockchain are numerous and they continue to increase at pace. Below are some of the key uses and associated areas of development.

13 https://www.theguardian.com/business/2018/mar/05/bitcoin-is-based-on-the-blockchain-pipe-dream.

14 https://www.pwc.com/gx/en/industries/technology/publications/blockchain-report-transform-business-economy.html.

15 https://www.businessinsider.com/blockchain-technology-applications-use-cases?r=US&IR=T.

1. *Smart contracts*

   The operation of smart contracts is discussed further below. In summary, blockchain-based smart contracts are automated self-executing pieces of code, that are either partially or completely executed on the occurrence of a specified event or fulfilment of certain criteria without human involvement. They do not require a third party to act as an intermediary between the contracting parties. The blockchain network executes the contract through automation. An example application could be in the context of insurance, whereby customers and insurers manage claims in a transparent and secure manner with all contracts and claims recorded on the blockchain and validated on the network. This has the potential to prevent invalid claims, for example, if the blockchain rejected multiple claims in relation to the same accident. By way of example, OpenIDL, a network built on the IBM Blockchain Platform with the American Association of Insurance Services is automating insurance regulatory reporting and streamlining compliance requirements.[16]

2. *Cryptocurrencies*

   Most cryptocurrencies including, for example, Bitcoin and Ethereum, use blockchain as its underlying technology and means of recording transactions.

3. *Financial services*

   Blockchain and DLT is being most enthusiastically explored in the context of financial services where it has potential to enhance efficiency, reliability, and security for a number of infrastructures and participants.

   According to *Reason*, many banks have expressed interest in implementing distributed ledgers for use in the sector and they are working with companies to create private blockchains.[17] As early as 2016, banks including UBS were opening research labs with a view to exploring how blockchain can be exploited in financial services.[18]

   In terms of money and payments, many financial institutions are exploring the implementation of blockchain systems in the context of payment authorisation, clearance, and settlement, foreign exchange, and micropayments. It has also been adopted for international payment transactions. For an example of the latter, in April 2018, Banco Santander launched the world's first blockchain-based money transfer service known as Santander One Pay FX. Santander describes this service as 'the world's first blockchain-inspired, multi-corridor international payments solution'. According to *Insider* Intelligence, it uses Ripple's xCurrent to allow the bank's customers to make same-day or next-day international money transfers.[19]

---

16 https://www.insiderintelligence.com/insights/blockchain-technology-applications-use-cases/.

17 https://reason.com/video/2016/05/06/bitcoin-consensus-blockchain-wall-street/.

18 https://www.reuters.com/article/us-banks-blockchain-ubs-idUSKCN10Z147.

19 https://www.insiderintelligence.com/insights/blockchain-technology-applications-use-cases/.

Blockchains also have the potential to restyle the capital markets industry, with significant impact on business models, reductions in risk and savings of cost and capital. In this context, blockchain technology can be applied to digital issuance, trading, and the settlement of securities, as well as commodities trading. It can also be used in a series of collateral services and particularly for registration (eg of securities, and for land registries).

In terms of internal adoption, businesses across various sectors are exploring the use of blockchain to replace internal ledgers that record information across different departments, geographies, and/or multi-entity corporate groups.

4. *Business/Supply chain*

As has been suggested above, blockchains can assist in supply-chain management, particularly in relation to tracking and management of inventory. It can also be used to establish product provenance and authenticity, as well as intellectual property registration. It can also assist the logistics of trade, such as for invoicing, storing customer records, and trade finance.

5. *Government*

Blockchain also has potential applications for government, firstly in the context of digital identity platforms and the storing of records (eg births, marriages, deaths, residences, criminal records etc) as well as internal government record-keeping, and secondly in relation to voting systems. It is also being explored by tax authorities in the context of fraud.

6. *Legal profession*

According to Consensys (citing Clio's Legal Trands Report 2018), lawyers spend up to 48% of their time on administrative tasks, including transferring information between software and updating client trust ledgers.[20] Blockchain technology has the potential to streamline many processes in the legal industry, particularly in the context of transactional work. Clients may soon come to habitually digitally sign and immutably store their contractual agreements, implement smart contracts, and automate contract management. Blockchain can also be used in regulatory compliance, for example by sharing compliance data across stakeholders and with appropriate authorities. In a matrimonial finance context, perhaps the future will one day see smart contract-based financial orders that are self-executing?

## G. SMART CONTRACTS

**3.07** Reference has been made above to smart contracts. A smart contract is a self-executing transaction protocol or piece of computer code that consists of a set of predefined rules that are designed to automatically execute upon the occasion of a specific event or satisfaction of certain criteria.

---

[20] https://consensys.net/blockchain-use-cases/law/.

In other words, when X happens, Y will automatically happen, usually in absence of any human participation.

The term 'smart contract' was apparently coined in the 1990s by Nick Szabo, who used it to refer to a set of promises, specified in digital form, including protocols within which the parties perform on those promises. Szabo's 1997 paper 'The Idea of Smart Contracts' referred to the use of a vending machine to illustrate the underlying concept:

> 'Many kinds of contractual clauses (such as collateral, bonding, delineation of property rights, etc.) can be embedded in the hardware and software we deal with, in such a way as to make breach of contract expensive (if desired, sometimes prohibitively so) for the breacher. A canonical real-life example, which we might consider to be the primitive ancestor of smart contracts, is the humble vending machine. Within a limited amount of potential loss (the amount in the till should be less than the cost of breaching the mechanism), the machine takes in coins, and via a simple mechanism, which makes a freshman computer science problem in design with finite automata, dispense change and product according to the displayed price. The vending machine is a contract with bearer: anybody with coins can participate in an exchange with the vendor. The lockbox and other security mechanisms protect the stored coins and contents from attackers, sufficiently to allow profitable deployment of vending machines in a wide variety of areas.
>
> Smart contracts go beyond the vending machine in proposing to embed contracts in all sorts of property that is valuable and controlled by digital means. Smart contracts reference that property in a dynamic, often proactively enforced form, and provide much better observation and verification where proactive measures must fall short.'[21]

A modern application could be a trading protocol executed by a smart contract whereby, for example, certain shares are purchased without human involvement when those shares reach a pre-defined price. In practice, smart contracts can be used in most scenarios where the fulfilment of contractual obligations involves some form of process.

A key point to be aware of is that a smart contract is not necessarily *in itself* a contract enforceable at law. Some academics have posited that smart contracts are not in themselves legal agreements at all, but rather a means of performing an obligation that is associated with a separate legal contract.

In terms of the ingredients required to make a smart contract legally enforceable, these are the same as for any contract under English law: offer, acceptance, intention to create legal relations,

---

21 https://nakamotoinstitute.org/the-idea-of-smart-contracts/.

and consideration. If any of these elements are not present, a smart contract may remain effective insofar as it may effect a pre-defined automated process, but it is unlikely to constitute an enforceable legal contract. It has also been observed that there are additional factors that need to be taken into account when smart contracts are used, including certainty of computer language (coding), and effective security to thwart potential hackers.

As was the position with cryptoassets, the UK Jurisdictional Taskforce ('UKJT') in its 'Legal statement on cryptoassets and smart contracts' (November 2019) declined to attempt a legal definition of a smart contract and instead focussed on the automaticity which is the defining feature of a smart contract:

> 'As with cryptoassets, it is difficult, and unlikely to be useful, to try to formulate a precise definition of smart contracts and so we have again sought instead to identify what it is about them that may be legally novel or distinctive. The characteristic feature, in our view, is automaticity: a smart contract is performed, at least in part, automatically and without the need for, and in some cases without the possibility of, human intervention. That requires the terms of the contract to be recorded in computer-readable form, i.e. in code. Many smart contracts are embedded in a networked system that executes and enforces performance using the same techniques (cryptographic authentication, distributed ledgers, decentralisation, consensus) that we have already discussed in connection with cryptoassets.'[22]

The UKJT's statement contains useful discussion of many of the issues likely to arise in litigation where smart contracts are involved and warrants reading in full.

A key point raised in the statement is that automaticity does not mean dispensing with the traditional requirements of English contract law. Where the legal contract 'lies' will be a matter of analysis on a case-by-case basis. In the authors' view, it is usually going to be the case that the parties will have agreed to have been bound by what the computer code 'does', but that will often not capture the entirety of the parties' agreement. The UKJT's view is that the usual rules of contractual interpretation will apply to a smart contract under English law. It is routinely the case that term sheets or other documents accompanying smart contracts are drafted in order to ensure clarity of intention. However, that does not mean that the value of the smart contract process is lessened. Term sheets are usually brief and easily incorporated into the "smart" process.

Noteworthy blockchain platforms that are able to support smart contracts include Ethereum, Bitcoin, Polkadot, Solana, and EOS.

---

22 A pdf of the report is available at: https://technation.io/lawtech-uk-resources/#cryptoassets.

## H. NON-FUNGIBLE TOKENS

**3.08** While this work focuses on cryptocurrencies, a nod must be given to non-fungible tokens ('NFTs') which are another type of cryptoasset.

*An NFT is a unit of data that is stored on a blockchain that can be traded.*

NFTs are typically associated in popular culture with photographs, videos, art, and audio files. They differ from cryptocurrencies in that each token is a uniquely identifiable (where the former, such as Bitcoin, are fungible). NFTs each have a digital signature that make it impossible for NFTs to be exchanged on an equivalent basis.

An NFT is minted from digital objects that can represent tangible and intangible items. In the press this has usually focussed on art and collectibles, but even GIFs and tweets have formed the basis of NFTs. For example, Twitter co-founder Jack Dorsey sold his first ever tweet as an NFT for over £2 million.

NFTs are treated as a digital equivalent to a physical collector's item, but rather than receiving, for example, a physical artwork, the purchaser receives a digital file and exclusive ownership rights. Accordingly, an artist can sell an NFT of a work of art as a separate asset to their physical creation. As noted in *Forbes*, Nyan Cat, a 2011 GIF of a cat with a pop-tart body sold for almost £424,000 in February 2022, while celebrities such as Snoop Dog and Lindsay Lohan are releasing artwork and other unique memories as NFTs.[23] In the past year brands such as Gucci, Burberry, Balenciaga and Dolce & Gabbana have all experimented with NFTs. Meanwhile, Selfridges in London debuted a project with French Maison Paco Rabanne with a concept of '12 Unwearable Dresses' where 12 dress styles are available for purchase online as NFTs.[24]

NFTs are therefore speculative digital assets. As is the case with cryptocurrency, NFTs will be considered in financial remedy proceedings in the same way that other assets will. They, like cryptocurrencies, may also give rise to unique challenges. These are discussed in other parts of this work and include issues of disclosure and preservation of the asset, and valuation.

In the recent case of *Lavinia Deborah Osbourne v (1) Persons Unknown (2) Ozone Networks Inc. trading as Opensea*[25] (unreported, April 2022), the High Court of England and Wales ordered an urgent interim injunction in respect of two NFTs. The NFTs represented two unique digital

---

23 https://www.forbes.com/uk/advisor/investing/cryptocurrency/nft-non-fungible-token/.

24 https://www.forbes.com/sites/roxannerobinson/2022/04/30/fashion-retailers-and-luxury-amp-up-nft-activations-after-adopting-the-technology-last-year/?sh=12eb0087a167.

25 *Lavinia Deborah Osbourne v (1) Persons Unknown (2) Ozone Networks Inc. trading as Opensea* [2022] EWHC 1021 (Comm).

artworks from the Boss Beauties series removed from the claimant's MetaMask wallet without her knowledge or consent in January 2022. This is believed to be the first case of its kind. The judgment recognises the proprietary rights of NFT holders at a time when these cryptoassets are increasingly being misappropriated. At the return hearing on 31 March 2022, HHJ Pelling QC granted another injunction until further order.[26] The judgement states the following at [13]–[17]:

> '13. I am satisfied on the basis of the evidence available that the claimant has demonstrated a good arguable case that she has been defrauded of the non-fungible tokens to which she refers in her evidence. There is clearly going to be an issue at some stage as to whether non-fungible tokens constitute property for the purposes of the law of England and Wales, but I am satisfied on the basis of the submissions made on behalf of the claimant that there is at least a realistically arguable case that such tokens are to be treated as property as a matter of English law.
>
> 14. The other factor which is material to this claim is where such tokens are to be treated as being located as at the time when they were lost. As is apparent from the limited description I have already given, non-fungible tokens are in effect a stream of electrons resulting in a credit item to a crypto account. As such, insofar as they have a physical manifestation at all, that is likely to be where the servers relevant to the account are maintained. However, attempting to litigate issues such as this by reference to a concept as ethereal as that would be difficult or impossible.
>
> 15. Unsurprisingly, therefore, in a series of cases relating to crypto currency fraud, it has been consistently held that crypto assets, are to be treated as located at the place where the owner of them is domiciled. There is no reason at any rate at this stage to treat non fungible tokens in any other way, assuming for present purposes as I do that they are to be treated as property as a matter of English law.
>
> 16. This approach has been adopted in any number of cases, including at least two, if not three, decided by me. All these cases follow what Butcher J said in *Ion Science Ltd v Persons Unknown and others* (unreported) [2020] (Comm), a judgment delivered on 21 December 2020 in the Commercial Court, where at paragraph 15, Butcher J held that the lex situs of a crypto asset is the place where the person or company who owns it is domiciled, adopting the analysis contained in Professor Andrew Dickinson's book on crypto currencies and public and private law. I consider I should follow these cases in relation to the asset the subject of these proceedings. Therefore, and for these purposes, the claimant is to be treated as having had the non-fungible tokens in her possession in England by operation of that principle.'

As a general matter, while this variety of asset is referred to as a 'non-fungible token', in the authors' view a better description would be 'non-fungible asset'. Assets can be bought, sold, leased, licensed, insured, and used as collateral. There is currently a level of concern about NFTs over their potential for fraudulent use. Such concern is well-founded but the key, as always, is in the proper creation and documentation generated in the 'dropping' process.

Popular NFT marketplaces include OpenSea.io, Rarible, and Foundation.

---

[26] https://36group.co.uk/news/2022/4/landmark-nft-judgment.

For illustrative purposes, the following were the top five NFTs by value based on sales through to 18 December 2021.[27]

1. 'The Merge' by an artist called Pak was purchased by a syndicate of approximately 30,000 collectors on 2 December 2021 for the price of US$91.8 million.
2. 'Everydays – the First 500 Days' is the product of Mike Winklemann, an artist known as 'Beeple'. The JPG file represents numerous images created by the artist every day from 2007 onwards. This work of art has been said to have triggered the popular craze for NFTs. The NFT was purchased on 11 March 2021 by a Singapore-based cryptocurrency investor for US$69.3 million. It is understood that the asset was purchased in Ether.
3. 'Human One' is a physical and digital artwork described as a 'kinetic video sculpture'. It was purchased at auction in November 2021 for US$28.9 million.
4. 'CryptoPunk No. 7523' is one of a series of 10,000 NFTs that slightly differ. They were initially free but have since gained considerable resale value. This NFT sold for US$11.75 million.
5. 'CryptoPunk No. 3100' is another in the series referred to immediate above. It is part of the so-called alien CryptoPunk series which made it into the top-10 list after being purchased by a major shareholder of DraftKings for US$7.67 million.

27 https://seekingalpha.com/article/4482591-top-nft-tokens. N.B. This list changes frequently.

*Chapter 4*

# The cryptocurrency ecosystem



## A. INTRODUCTION

**4.01** As suggested in previous chapters of this work, the use and development of blockchains has soared in recent years and the number of cryptocurrencies has grown exponentially. Today's cryptocurrencies go far beyond simply providing an alternative to fiat currency. The new blockchain economy represents a financial ecosystem that is both revolutionary and evolutionary, as well as offering unique solutions in security, identification, and ownership, touching upon practically every sector. Over 18,000 cryptocurrencies are in existence as of March 2022. Though many of these cryptocurrencies have little to no following or trading volume, many lesser-known coins enjoy noteworthy popularity among small but highly enthusiastic communities of investors and backers.[1]

The cryptocurrency market is populated by various actors who play specific roles. This chapter identifies those 'key players' and explains certain key terms that practitioners need to be aware of when encountering cryptocurrencies in litigation.

This chapter also provides data and information on the current top 10 cryptocurrencies by market capitalisation. The information and data relating to those cryptocurrencies is current as of June 2022 and has been predominantly obtained from coinmarketcap.com.

---

1 https://www.investopedia.com/tech/most-important-cryptocurrencies-other-than-bitcoin/.

## B. KEY PLAYERS AND KEY TERMS

### i. Cryptocurrency users

**4.02** A 'cryptocurrency user' is a generic term referring to a natural person or entity who owns or obtains coins. These coins are usually used to: (i) purchase real or virtual goods or services from online merchants; (ii) to make person-to-person payments; or (iii) to hold them in a speculative manner as a means of investment.[2] As outlined in previous chapters, coins can be obtained by a cryptocurrency user in several ways, including the following:

- they can buy coins on a cryptocurrency exchange using fiat money or another cryptocurrency. This is the usual 'on ramp' method of acquiring cryptocurrency in the first instance;
- they can buy coins directly from another cryptocurrency user (ie through a trading platform – this form of exchange is often referred to as a 'P2P exchange');
- if a cryptocurrency is based on a proof of work consensus mechanism, they can mine a new coin (ie participate in the validation of transactions by the solving of a 'cryptographic puzzle' which results in being rewarded with new coin(s));
- in some cases, they can obtain coins directly from a coin offeror, either as part of a free initial offering of coins or in the framework of a crowd sale established by the coin offeror (eg a large bulk of ether (cf Ethereum) was sold in a crowd sale to cover development costs);
- if they sell goods or services in exchange for cryptocurrency, they can also receive coins as a payment for those goods or services;
- In the case of a 'hard fork' of a coin's blockchain, they acquiror will often automatically obtain an amount of the newly created coin; and
- they can receive coins as a gift or donation from another cryptocurrency user.[3]

### ii. Public and private keys

**4.03** As explained in Chapter 2, public key cryptography is a cryptographic system which uses a pair of 'keys' consisting of a public key and a private key.

A public key is a piece of cryptographic code that allows users to receive cryptocurrencies into their accounts.

---

2 'Cryptocurrencies and Blockchain Report' of the European Parliament, Policy Department for Economic, Scientific and Quality of Life Policies (Prof. Dr. Robby Houben, Alexander Snyers), PE 619.024 July 2018, at p 25.

3 Ibid.

The public key and private key are the tools which together ensure the security of the cryptographic system.

When a cryptocurrency user undertakes their first transaction, a unique public key and a private key are created. Each of the keys consists of a strand of alphanumeric characters. The private key is known to only the user and effectively constitutes that individual's digital identification. The private key authorises the user to transact with or handle the assets held in the relevant account. A sophisticated algorithm is applied to the private key so as to generate a public key, and both keys are stored in a digital wallet (as to which, see further below).

It is important for practitioners to be aware that a private key can take one of many forms:

- 256 character long binary code;
- 64-digit hexadecimal code;
- QR code;
- Mnemonic phrase.

By way of example, in one format, a public and a private key can look like this:

```
n = 2245944838578036526972583396448350551747843525119085870865837921064767862499
    5080698551937025022186301711535333198664798188326624882731471433305369620049
    9826334796240761090584167633432656265188647836110242553974179632080636660650
    9553493655928231758714894373780618182801915185644831114898975050468805964483
    6329930121323954250397233617250981771294652550666361750227000001163814082240
    1213802131566884820219731159073117564151470164344800066475416917008836012841
    6453999693815862274498910264041949675057120833402528603066416796403657742578
    8899951399542059233818410379611323656680403814378526886221231167479535046352
    291836079

e = 65537
d = 5438629261063741044456551032490856044103067998785402562009376048231970639160
    6562809713481024017287426669219790021333040457870140056601378098868763579381
    6049549600430425333410247698639891195590863353383516079706155417721242016651
    7633389431860023804996471262324856273718112516011332498198992027547789898279
    6367125516774011214449348835105146112524832528466786061288886908728901871761
    7330798675702944198764135596823504891287070715575597029612982520978737317421
    9386789071135476909410835408405212931007402450771425225993435533102280382944
    3362040358826807748069982321379309636762497447239054568638341393733053187204
    3814049
```

In this example, the public key is made up of the modulus *n*, and the public (or encryption) exponent *e*. The private key is made up of the modulus *n* and the private (or decryption) exponent *d*, which must be kept secret.[4]

---

[4] Example from: https://kulkarniamit.github.io/whatwhyhow/security/public-key-cryptography.html.

In Bitcoin, a private key is a 256-bit number. Here is an example private key in hexadecimal – 256 bits in hexadecimal is 32 bytes, or 64 characters in the range 0–9 or A–F.[5]

```
E9873D79C6D87DC0FB6A5778633389F4453213303DA61F20BD67FC233AA33262
```

The transaction process using the public and private keys is briefly summarised as follows:

- When a transaction is initiated, the transaction is first broadcast to the network where distributed nodes will confirm the validity of the transaction before completing it and recording the transaction on the blockchain.
- Prior to broadcast, the transaction is digitally signed by the user using their private key. This key proves ownership without revealing details of the private key or individual to anyone else. The public key is used to prove that the digital signature came from the individual's private key. Once the transaction has been verified by the network as valid, the transaction (eg, transfer of coins) takes place and the coins are sent to the recipient individual's public address.
- When two individuals transact and one sends the other coins, they reveal their public addresses to each other. The public address is the equivalent of a bank account number. The transferring party needs to know the number to be able to send the coins to the recipient. The recipient party will then be able to spend or withdraw those coins using their private key. They will also be able to verify the sender's batch of coins using the sender's public address.[6]

The key point to be aware of when it comes to litigation, including in a matrimonial finance context, is that *access and control of the data which constitutes the cryptoasset is fundamental to the control, tracing, and dealing with the cryptoasset itself.* It follows that if, for example, the private key is unknown or lost, then access to the cryptoassets is similarly lost.

### iii. Wallets and wallet providers

**4.04** A wallet is typically software or an application or physical device that stores the public and/or private keys that facilitate cryptocurrency transactions. In addition, wallets often facilitate the signing and/or encrypting of data.

It should be borne in mind that the 'wallet' does not hold cash or the cryptocurrency itself, but rather the keys needed to execute transactions whilst also providing the interface that allows the individual to access cryptocurrency.

---

5 Example from: https://en.bitcoin.it/wiki/Private_key.

6 https://www.investopedia.com/terms/p/public-key.asp.

Wallets contain the public key (the wallet address) and the private key needed to sign a transaction. Anybody who knows the private key can control the assets associated with that address.

There are two main varieties of wallet: *custodial* and *non-custodial.* The former is hosted by a third party which stores the keys on the individual's behalf. Non-custodial wallets are wallets which the individual has control over (and therefore the responsibility for securing the keys). Most cryptocurrency wallets on devices are non-custodial wallets.

Of these types of wallet there are two sub-categories: *hot wallets* and *cold wallets.* A hot wallet requires a connection to the internet and a cold wallet does not. Of these two varieties, the wallets can be sub-categorised as *software, hardware, and paper wallets* (with all but the latter being a hot or a cold wallet). Accordingly, it is possible to have a noncustodial software hot wallet, a noncustodial hardware cold or hot wallet, or a custodial hardware cold wallet.[7]

*The key point to note is that a holder of cryptocurrency uses private keys to access the cryptocurrency. Anybody who has that private key can access the coins. If the private key is lost or cannot be located, the coins cannot be accessed.*

When dealing with cryptocurrency in a matrimonial finance case, it is important to be aware of the fact that a wallet can take one of many forms. On the one hand, it could be an application on a phone connecting to an online exchange, on the other it could simply be a strip of paper held in a safe. Often, they are held on USB devices. There may also be multiple copies of a private key held in more than one place – anybody who has access to that private key will be able to deal with the asset. This should be kept in mind if steps are needed to preserve the asset, perhaps by way of a freezing order (see Chapter 8). Equally, the private key could simply be memorised by a party.

Popular providers of crypto wallets include: Coinbase Wallet; Electrum; Mycelium; Ledger Nano X, Exodus, and Crypto.com.[8]

### iv. Miners

**4.05** As outlined in Chapter 3, an important figure in the cryptocurrency landscape is the 'miner'.

This is a type of participant (node) who validates transactions on the blockchain by solving a mathematically complex cryptographic puzzle. This is a feature of cryptocurrencies that use the proof of work consensus mechanism.

7 https://www.investopedia.com/terms/b/bitcoin-wallet.asp.
8 https://money.com/best-crypto-wallets/.

A miner contributes substantial computing power to perform the validation and receives a reward in the form of newly minted coins.

Miners can be cryptocurrency users in their own right, or they can perform the function as part of a business enterprise. Cryptocurrency solo miners will usually have specialist hardware. Mining with a graphics processing unit or an application specific integrated circuit is considered to be the most effective, although everyday desktop computers can also be used. As referred to below, the process of mining is resource-intensive in terms of bandwidth availability and power. It requires enormous amounts of electricity.

According to *thebalance.com*,

> 'the Bitcoin network, which includes miners, nodes, and Bitcoin users, consumes more energy than many countries. As of January 16, 2022, the Bitcoin network consumes 131.00 TWh (that's terawatt-hours) of electricity annually, meaning that Bitcoin uses more electricity than countries such as Norway and the Ukraine, and a little less than Egypt and Poland.'[9]

In terms of the Bitcoin blockchain, the validation of a block currently provides a reward of 6.25 bitcoins, which is currently worth approximately £156,000. Miners can work in isolation, but they often form syndicate 'mining pools' to share rewards.

## v. Exchanges

**4.06** A cryptocurrency exchange is an organisation or entity that offers exchange services to cryptocurrency users, usually in return for payment of commission. They allow participants to deal or transact with their cryptocurrencies and/or to exchange them for fiat currency.

Exchanges also allow individuals to buy cryptocurrency with fiat currency. This is often the 'on ramp' where an individual will acquire cryptocurrency for the first time. *It is for this reason that it is important to review financial disclosure for any transactions involving exchanges, noting that these transfers may be for very modest sums.* Such transactions could indicate that at some point the individual has had a cryptocurrency holding of some variety.

Care should be taken when debits or credits from an exchange are identified. Given the volatility and growth of cryptoassets such as Bitcoin identified in previous chapters, an initial transfer of, eg £50 to Coinbase, could be a clue – perhaps the only clue – in relation to what thereafter became a substantial holding of cryptocurrency. The client will need to be advised as to what further disclosure or preservatory steps are needed at that stage.

---

9 https://www.thebalance.com/how-does-bitcoin-mining-work-5088328.

In terms of how exchanges work practically, an individual cannot at present purchase cryptocurrency using their traditional high street banks or investing firms. When they want to acquire Ether or another cryptocurrency, they will need to create an online account on an exchange which will allow the exchange of fiat currency for cryptoassets.

Popular exchanges include: Coinbase, Crypto.com, Kraken, Binance, and Gemini.

Note that some cryptocurrency exchanges also operate as custodian wallet providers (eg Bitfinex). Equally, some operate as *pure* cryptocurrency exchanges and do not accept payments in fiat currency. More often than not, cryptocurrency exchanges offer payment options covering most fiat currencies as well as PayPal and its equivalents, and credit cards.

### vi. Coin inventors and offerors

**4.07** As its name suggests, a coin inventor is the person or group of people who develop the underlying technology that supports a cryptocurrency. Most notably, the inventors of Bitcoin and Monero are unidentified, while for Cardano, Ripple, Litecoin and more recent cryptocurrencies, the inventors' identities are known. Many remain actively involved in the maintenance of the currency's code and algorithm (in principle without administrator's powers).[10]

By contrast, coin offerors are individuals or organisations that offer coins to cryptocurrency users upon a coin's initial release. This is offered either for payment (a crowd sale) or at no charge as part and parcel of a sign-up program. This is often undertaken to fund the coin's further development or to enhance its popularity from the point of launch. The coins offered are created or pre-mined prior to the coin's official release. It is important to note that not all coins have an identifiable coin offeror, and nor are all coins pre-mined or at full supply prior to the launch.[11]

## C. TOP 10 CRYPTOCURRENCIES BY MARKET CAPITALISATION: BITCOIN, ETHEREUM, TETHER, USD COIN, BNB, CARDANO, XRP, BINANCE USD, SOLANA, DOGECOIN

**4.08** The remainder of this chapter provides information on the current top 10 cryptocurrencies by market capitalisation. Given their primacy, these are the cryptocurrencies that are most likely to be encountered in the course of litigation (though of course, the list is subject to frequent change).

---

10 'Cryptocurrencies and Blockchain Report' of the European Parliament, Policy Department for Economic, Scientific and Quality of Life Policies (Prof. Dr. Robby Houben, Alexander Snyers), PE 619.024 July 2018, at p 28.

11 Ibid.

It is important to have a basic understanding of the cryptoasset in question because different cryptocurrencies have different features and underlying technologies, price histories, and degrees of volatility. Some may be experiencing turbulence or rapidly gaining (or losing) value, while others are ostensibly static. Tether Gold (XAUT) and USD Coin (USDC), for example, by their very nature behave differently to, say, Bitcoin or Cardano. This can impact an approach to valuation in the proceedings, and, conceivably, a client's (or the Court's) willingness to premise a settlement based on offsetting the cryptocurrency against another type of asset.

*The information and data set out below is current as of June 2022 and has been obtained from coinmarketcap.com or the whitepaper or website associated with the relevant cryptocurrency.* The global crypto market cap is currently US$1.21 trillion.

**1. Bitcoin (BTC)**

| | |
|---|---|
| **Price** | US$29,152.65 |
| **Market dominance** | 45.81% |
| **Market rank** | 1 |
| **Market cap** | US$556,061,978,675.88 |
| **Fully diluted market cap** | US$612,888,633,353.13 |
| **All-time high** | US$68,789.63 |
| **All-time low** | US$65.53 |
| **Circulating supply** | 19,052,893 BTC |
| **Max supply** | 21,000,000 BTC |

**What Is Bitcoin (BTC)?**

As described in Chapter 2, Bitcoin is a decentralised cryptocurrency originally theorised in the 2008 white paper by a person, or group of people, known by the alias 'Satoshi Nakamoto'. The currency was launched in January 2009.

Bitcoin is peer-to-peer, which means that all Bitcoin transactions are effected between equal network participants without the need for any third party intermediary.

Bitcoin operates on a permissionless public blockchain. It was created, according to Nakamoto, in order to facilitate 'online payments to be sent directly from one party to another without going through a financial institution'.

Bitcoin is known as being the first-ever cryptocurrency to come into circulation. It remains the most well-known digital currency.

**The origin of Bitcoin**

As suggested above and in Chapter 2, very little is known about the original inventor of Bitcoin, who is referred to by the pseudonym, Satoshi Nakamoto. We do not know who this person, or persons, may be. It could be an alias for a group of hackers. This question has lent a popular mystique to the oldest cryptocurrency in circulation.

Bitcoin's white paper was published on 31 October 2008. This document sets out in detail the theoretical basis for a peer-to-peer decentralised online currency. The white paper describes how a decentralised ledger of transactions could be accumulated into 'blocks' and secured by cryptography. This is the revolutionary system that would later be referred to by the moniker, 'blockchain'. On 3 January 2009, Nakamoto mined the initial 'genesis' block which would launch the cryptocurrency. At that point in time, most Bitcoins were obtained via the process of mining (see Chapter 2). Its price at that point of introduction was US$0. The first recorded commercial transaction using Bitcoin took place on 22 May 2010 when Laszlo Hanyecz traded 10,000 Bitcoins for two pizzas. At that price, the coins exchanged for those pizzas would today be worth several hundred million pounds. In July 2010, Bitcoin commenced trading, with its price ranging from roughly US$0.0008 to US$0.08.

While the alias referred to as 'Satoshi Nakamoto' was the inventor of Bitcoin, as well as the author of the white paper setting out its conceptual basis and method of implementation, the network alert key and control of the code repository was subsequently passed to Gavin Andresen. Anderson later became the Bitcoin Foundation's lead developer. In the years that followed, a variety of other individuals came on board and developed the cryptocurrency's software, including developing the algorithm to add new features and patch susceptibilities as they arose. According to *coinmarketcap.com*, Bitcoin's source code repository on GitHub identifies more than 750 contributors, with some of the key individuals being Wladimir J van der Laan, Marco Falke, Pieter Wuille, Gavin Andresen, Jonas Schnelli among others.

**Bitcoin's unique features**

The advantage that Bitcoin has over other cryptocurrencies in the market derives from the fact that it was the first cryptocurrency.

Since its inception it has accumulated an enormous global fanbase and is now synonymous with cryptocurrency as a concept. Millions of fans create, trade, and speculate with Bitcoin. It has also been said that Bitcoin's growth has spurred on thousands of competing cryptocurrency projects. As of May 2022, it is believed that there are more than 18,000 cryptocurrencies in circulation. The entire cryptocurrency market – at the time of writing worth approximately US$1.2 trillion – is founded on the initial idea arising out of Satoshi Nakamoto's white paper, that of a digital currency that can function on a peer-to-peer basis using a decentralised model without reliance on any third-party intermediaries.

Despite its age and, arguably, the increasingly visible limitations of its underlying technology, Bitcoin continues to dominate the market, holding a total market dominance of approximately 46%. It is the largest cryptocurrency: in 2021 its market capitalisation passed the US$1 trillion mark. It high an all-time price high of $64,863.10 on 14 April 2021. Analysts have said that this growth and continued dominance of the market is owed to the unique institutional interest in Bitcoin.

A further unique feature of Bitcoin is the fact that its total supply is limited by its own software: it can never exceed 21,000,000 coins.

As described in Chapter 2, new Bitcoins are created via a process known as 'mining'. This is where transactions are broadcast across the market, which are then taken-up by miner nodes and become packaged into 'blocks' which are secured by a process known as cryptography. Miners are provided with rewards in the form of coins for every block that they add to the blockchain. This is a form of reward for the expenditure of high levels of computational resources and energy. According to *coinmarketcap.com*, at the point of Bitcoin's launch, the reward was 50 bitcoins per block. This number is halved with every 210,000 new blocks mined, which takes the network roughly four years. As of 2020, the block reward has been halved three times and comprises 6.25 bitcoins (worth approximately £165,000 at the time of writing).

No Bitcoins are mined and/or distributed among the cryptocurrency's founders before they are made available to the public at large.

During the first years of the cryptocurrency's existence, the competition for rewards was relatively low which meant that the first wave of participants were able to acquire large numbers of coins via mining. It is believed that 'Satoshi Nakamoto' alone possesses over a million Bitcoin, though we do not know who Nakamoto may be or whether the individual(s) behind the pseudonym are still alive. The result is that the process of mining is potentially lucrative, depending on the current hash rate and the price of the cryptoasset.

**How Is Bitcoin's network secured?**

Bitcoin is secured with the SHA-256 algorithm, which belongs to the SHA-2 family of hashing algorithms, which is also used by its fork Bitcoin Cash (BCH) as well as several other cryptocurrencies.

**Issues of energy consumption**

There has been increasing international concern about Bitcoin and energy usage.

Research has suggested that each Bitcoin transaction takes 1,173 KW hours of electricity, which can 'power the typical American home for six weeks'. Another report has calculated that the energy required by Bitcoin annually is more than the annual hourly energy usage of Finland. Miners are increasingly reliant on renewable energy sources, with estimates suggesting that Bitcoin's use of renewable energy may span anywhere from 40–75%. However, critics claim that increasing Bitcoin's renewable energy usage will take away from solar sources powering other sectors and industries.

**Units of value**

The smallest units of Bitcoin, 0.00000001 BTC, are called Satoshis (or Sats in short), in a reference to its creator. For many, Bitcoin is considered a store of value, like assets such as gold, rather than a currency. It is therefore perceived as having speculative value as an asset to be held on a medium to long-term basis.

**Wallets for Bitcoin**

As identified above, cryptocurrency wallets can be hot and cold. Hot wallets are those which are connected to the internet, while cold wallets facilitate the holding of coins outside of the internet. Notable cold wallets are Trezor, Ledger and CoolBitX, while hot wallets include Exodus, Electrum and Mycelium.

**The value of Bitcoin**

Bitcoin's value fluctuates daily. Starting with a value of under one cent per coin, at its highest it was worth US$65,789.63. One of the issues addressed in Chapter 8 is that of volatility which to varying degrees impact all types of cryptoassets. This is exacerbated by the fact that different countries and exchanges may present a different price for Bitcoin simultaneously.

**Where is Bitcoin acquired?**

As suggested above, one way in which Bitcoin can be acquired is by mining. However, it is anticipated that in most matrimonial finance cases it will, like other cryptoassets, be purchased by a party (in the first instance, with fiat currency or other cryptocurrencies).

Given Bitcoin's primacy, it is available to purchase on practically every crypto exchange.

Markets where Bitcoin is traded include: Binance, Coinbase Pro, OKEx, and Kraken.

As has been explained in other parts of this work, Bitcoin is the paradigm 'exchange token'. The regulation of different types of token is considered in Chapter 5.

## 2. Ethereum

| | |
|---|---|
| **Price** | US$1,860.33 |
| **Market dominance** | 17.65% |
| **Market rank** | 2 |
| **Market cap** | US$225,235,324,000.06 |
| **Fully diluted market cap** | US$225,235,324,000.06 |
| **All-time high** | US$4,891.70 |
| **All-time low** | US$0.4209 |
| **Circulating supply** | 121,072,541 ETH |
| **Max supply** | – |

### What Is Ethereum (ETH)?

Ethereum is a decentralised open-source blockchain system that features its own cryptocurrency, known as Ether. ETH operates as a platform for numerous other cryptocurrencies, as well as for the execution of decentralized smart contracts.

Ethereum was first propounded in Vitalik Buterin's 2013 white paper:[12]

> 'Satoshi Nakamoto's development of Bitcoin in 2009 has often been hailed as a radical development in money and currency, being the first example of a digital asset which simultaneously has no backing or "intrinsic value" and no centralized issuer or controller. However, another, arguably more important, part of the Bitcoin experiment is the underlying blockchain technology as a tool of distributed consensus, and attention is rapidly starting to shift to this other aspect of Bitcoin. Commonly cited alternative applications of blockchain technology include using on-blockchain digital assets to represent custom currencies and financial instruments ("colored coins"), the ownership of an underlying physical device ("smart property"), non-fungible assets such as domain names ("Namecoin"), as well as more complex applications involving having digital assets being directly controlled by a piece of code implementing arbitrary rules ("smart contracts") or even blockchain-based "decentralized autonomous organizations" (DAOs). What Ethereum intends to provide is a blockchain with a built-in fully fledged Turing-complete programming language that can be used to create "contracts" that can be used to encode arbitrary state transition functions, allowing users to create any of the systems described above, as well as many others that we have not yet imagined, simply by writing up the logic in a few lines of code.'
>
> […]
>
> 'The Ethereum protocol was originally conceived as an upgraded version of a cryptocurrency, providing advanced features such as on-blockchain escrow, withdrawal limits, financial contracts, gambling markets and the like via a highly generalized programming language. The Ethereum protocol would not "support" any of the applications directly, but the existence of

12 https://ethereum.org/en/whitepaper/#a-next-generation-smart-contract-and-decentralized-application-platform.

> a Turing-complete programming language means that arbitrary contracts can theoretically be created for any transaction type or application. What is more interesting about Ethereum, however, is that the Ethereum protocol moves far beyond just currency. Protocols around decentralized file storage, decentralized computation and decentralized prediction markets, among dozens of other such concepts, have the potential to substantially increase the efficiency of the computational industry, and provide a massive boost to other peer-to-peer protocols by adding for the first time an economic layer. Finally, there is also a substantial array of applications that have nothing to do with money at all.
>
> The concept of an arbitrary state transition function as implemented by the Ethereum protocol provides for a platform with unique potential; rather than being a closed-ended, single-purpose protocol intended for a specific array of applications in data storage, gambling or finance, Ethereum is open-ended by design, and we believe that it is extremely well-suited to serving as a foundational layer for a very large number of both financial and non-financial protocols in the years to come.'

The project was funded by a crowd sale in 2014 which raised US$18.3 million in Bitcoin. Ethereum's price in its initial coin offering was US$0.311, with over 60 million Ether sold. Applying Ethereum's current price, this puts the return on investment at an annualised rate of over 270%, almost quadrupling an initial investment every year since the summer of 2014.

The Ethereum Foundation officially launched the blockchain on 30 July 2015 under a prototype codenamed 'Frontier'. Several network updates have followed, namely 'Constantinople' on 28 February 2019, 'Istanbul' on 8 December 2019, 'Muir Glacier' on 2 January 2020, 'Berlin' on 14 April 2021, and the 'London' hard fork on 5 August 2021.

Ethereum had numerous co-founders: Vitalik Buterin, Gavin Wood, Anthony Di Iorio, Charles Hoskinson, Mihai Alisie, Joseph Lubin, and Amir Chetrit. Ethereum's stated intention is to become a global platform for decentralised applications.

**Ethereum's unique features**

As suggested above in the white paper referenced above, Ethereum first propounded the concept of a blockchain smart contract platform.

The key innovation of Ethereum was to design a platform that allowed it to execute smart contracts using the blockchain, which reinforced the increasingly recognised benefits of smart contract technology. According to co-founder Gavin Wood, the intention was to create 'one computer for the entire planet', theoretically able to make any program more robust, censorship-resistant, and less vulnerable to fraud by operating it simultaneously across a distributed network all over the world.

Ethereum's blockchain can also host other cryptocurrencies, and not just Ether. This is facilitated by the ERC-20 compatibility standard. According to *coinmarketcap.com*, this is the most common use for the ETH platform: to date, more than 280,000 ERC-20-compliant tokens have been launched using Ethereum's blockchain. Over 40 of these make the top-100 cryptocurrencies by market capitalisation.

Ethereum has historically been troubled by high transaction fees, often struggling during seasons of high demand. In May 2021, the average transaction fee of the network peaked at US$71.72. In addition to the high transaction costs, it also suffers from scalability limitations. The transition process to ETH 2.0 has already begun with some upgrades having been implemented including the 'London' hard fork which went live in August 2021. The movement to ETH 2.0 has been part of Ethereum's plans since its inception. The current Ethereum chain will become the Beacon Chain and will provide a settlement layer for smart contract interactions on other chains.

**Ethereum (ETH) in circulation**

As of September 2021, there were around 117.5 million ETH coins in circulation, 72 million of which were issued in the Ethereum blockchain's genesis block. Of the 72 million, 60 million were allocated to initial participants in the 2014 crowd sale and 12 million were given to the development fund. The remainder has been issued in block rewards to miners. In 2015 the block reward was five ETH per block. This was subsequently reduced to two ETH in early 2019.

In the August 2021 network upgrade, the 'London' hard fork contained an improvement protocol (EIP-1559). This protocol replaced a first-price auction mechanism with a 'base fee' for transactions to be included in successive blocks. Users that want to have their transaction prioritised can pay a 'priority fee' to miners.

One of the major differences between Bitcoin and Ethereum's economics is that the total supply of the latter is not limited. The ability to adjust the issuance rate via consensus allows the network to maintain the minimum issuance needed for adequate security.

**How Is the Ethereum Network Secured?**

As of August 2020, Ethereum was secured via the Ethash proof-of-work algorithm. The subsequent Ethereum 2.0 update included plans to transition the network to a proof-of-stake algorithm. Following the launch of the Ethereum 2.0 Beacon Chain (Phase 0) in December 2020, it became possible to begin staking on the Ethereum 2.0 network. An Ethereum stake is when you deposit ETH (32 ETH is required to activate validator software) on Ethereum

2.0 by sending it to a deposit contract, thus helping to secure the network by storing data, processing transactions, and adding new blocks to the blockchain. Ethereum staking rewards are determined by a distribution curve (the participation and average percent of stakers): some ETH 2.0 staking rewards were at 20% for early stakers but this will apparently be lowered to end up between 7% and 4.5% annually. The minimum requirements for an Ethereum stake are 32 ETH.

**Where is Ethereum (ETH) acquired?**

Given its size and market rank, Ethereum can be bought on all major exchanges (eg Binance, Coinbase Pro, Kraken etc). it is possible to use ETH trading pairs on nearly all of the major crypto exchanges.

Ether is a variety of token. The regulation of different types of token is considered in Chapter 5.

**3. Tether**

| | |
|---|---|
| **Price** | US$0.9993 |
| **Market dominance** | 5.68% |
| **Market rank** | 3 |
| **Market cap** | US$72,499,016,124.78 |
| **Fully diluted market cap** | US$79,664,797,445.29 |
| **All-time high** | US$1.22 |
| **All-time low** | US$0.5683 |
| **Circulating supply** | 72,543,449,553 USDT |
| **Max supply** | – |

**What Is Tether (USDT)?**

Launched in 2014, Tether tokens pioneered the stablecoin model and are the most widely traded token of that variety. Tether tokens purport to offer the stability and simplicity of fiat currencies such as sterling and the US dollar coupled with the benefits of blockchain technology.

USDT is a stablecoin that mirrors the price of the US dollar. The token's peg to the US dollar is achieved by maintaining an assessed quantity of commercial paper, fiduciary deposits, cash, reserve repo notes, and treasury bills in reserves that equal in US dollar value the number of USDT in circulation. The regulation of stablecoins is considered in Chapter 5.

The cryptocurrency was originally launched in 2014 under the name Realcoin, which was a second-layer cryptocurrency token built on Bitcoin's blockchain. The currency was later renamed USTether, and then, finally, to USDT. In addition to Bitcoin's blockchain, USDT has subsequently been updated to operate on the Ethereum, EOS, Tron, Algorand, and OMG blockchains.

USDT moves across the blockchain just as easily as other digital currencies but its tokens are pegged to real-world (ie fiat) currencies on a 1-to-1 basis. According to Tether, this offers traders, merchants, and funds a low volatility proposition when exiting positions in the market. All Tether tokens are pegged at 1-to-1 with a matching fiat currency (eg, 1 USDT = 1 USD) and are backed 100% by Tether's reserves.[13]

Tether tokens exist as digital tokens built on various blockchains including Algorand, Ethereum, EOS, Liquid Network, Omni, Tron, Bitcoin Cash's Standard Ledger Protocol, and Solana. Therefore, issuance of Tether tokens is viable on various blockchains with varying capabilities depending on the transport protocol used.

Tether tokens have grown in popularity over the past few years, with a market cap of over US$77 billion (as of December 2021). Tether promotes its tokens on the basis that they allow purchasers the ability to transact across different blockchains without the inherent volatility and complexity typically associated with digital tokens.[14]

Realcoin was launched in 2014 by Brock Pierce, Reeve Collins and Craig Sellars.

**Tether's unique features**

USDT's unique feature is its main function: its value is guaranteed by Tether to remain pegged to the US dollar. According to Tether, whenever it issues new USDT tokens, it allocates the same amount of USD to its reserves. This means that USDT is fully backed by cash and cash equivalents. Tether asserts that it only issues new Tether tokens when they are requested by customers who have followed strict KYC procedures.

The result is that USDT is insulated from the capricious volatility experienced by the crypto market. During periods of instability, crypto holders have transferred their portfolios into Tether or similar coins so as to avoid having to cash-out into fiat currency. As Tether highlights on its website, USDT also provides a means of effectively transacting with an equivalent to the US dollar between geographies via blockchain and without a third-party intermediary (and associated costs).

As noted on *coinmarketcap.com*, there have been various controversies over the years regarding Tether's assertions about its US dollar reserves. It highlights that there has never been a full audit of Tether's reserves by an independent third party.

13 https://tether.to/en/how-it-works.
14 Ibid.

**Tether (USDT) in circulation**

Given that USDT belongs to a private company its issuance is determined by its own policies. Accordingly, there is no limit on its total supply written into its code. However, in line with Tether's own stated policy that every USDT (coin) is backed to one US dollar, the amount of tokens would theoretically remain limited to the number amount of cash held in reserve by the company.

Note that Tether does not provide advance issuance schedules but rather provides transparency reports that list the total amount of their asset reserves and liabilities.

According to *coinmarketcap.com*, as of September 2020, there were more than 14.4 billion USDT tokens in circulation, which were accordingly backed by US$14.6 billion in assets (according to Tether).

**How Is the Tether Network Secured?**

USDT does not operate on its own blockchain. It functions as a second-layer token resting on other blockchains: Bitcoin, Ethereum, EOS, Tron, Algorand, Bitcoin Cash and OMG. It is therefore secured by their respective hashing algorithms.

**Where is Tether (USDT) acquired?**

USDT is available on many exchanges. According to *coinmarketcap.com*, USDT's average daily trading volume is often on par or even exceeds that of Bitcoin. It is particularly popular on exchanges where fiat-to-crypto trading pairs are not available.

Some of the more popular exchanges supporting Tether include: Binance, OKEx, and Huobi Global.

**4. USD Coin**

| | |
|---|---|
| **Price** | US$1.00 |
| **Market dominance** | 4.22% |
| **Market rank** | 4 |
| **Market cap** | US53,818,564,178.42 |
| **Fully diluted market cap** | US$53,818,564,178.42 |
| **All-time high** | US$2.35 |
| **All-time low** | US$0.9292 |
| **Circulating supply** | 53,809,633,081 USDC |
| **Max supply** | – |

USD Coin (known as USDC) is a stablecoin that was brought to market by Circle and Coinbase.

It is an open source, smart contract-based stable coin that is pegged to the US dollar on a 1:1 basis. Every unit of USDC in circulation is backed up by US$1 that is held in reserve in a mix of cash and short-term US Treasury bonds. The CENTRE consortium, which is behind this asset, says USDC is issued by regulated financial institutions.

According to CENTRE's white paper:[15]

> 'In addition to governing and auditing network membership, CENTRE plans to provide technology to address price volatility and transaction scalability challenges on top of existing public blockchain infrastructure. Specifically, CENTRE plans to provide:
>
> - A mechanism for issuing members to mint and burn/redeem asset-backed fiat tokens, or "stablecoins," to address price volatility;
> - Protocols to enable global stablecoin transaction interoperability on public blockchains using state channels for increased throughput and scalability;
> - Network membership rules and smart contracts to govern, audit, and manage the licensed network participants that mint, transact, and redeem stablecoins.
>
> [...]
>
> In addition to transactional use cases involving global payments, stablecoins issued by CENTRE network members also aim to address key use cases involving crypto asset exchange risk.
>
> Crypto asset exchanges are online marketplaces in which buyers and sellers come together to trade crypto assets such as bitcoin, ethereum, and others. These crypto assets fluctuate in price according to the market. Tokenized fiat money, such as tokenized US dollars, does not fluctuate in value, but rather remains price-pegged to the value of its underlying backing asset (in this example, the value of one tokenized US dollar is always intended to be priced at one US fiat dollar).
>
> This makes price-stable tokens useful for providing fiat connectivity and for hedging risk on crypto exchanges, particularly on those exchanges that do not provide traditional fiat on- and off-ramps – so long as the price truly is stable, and so long as there are compliant protections around the minting and redemption of such tokens. A hypothetical investor may choose to protect himself from bitcoin's fluctuating value by trading his bitcoin for US dollar tokens on a supporting exchange, and be certain that the value of those US dollar tokens will not fluctuate.
>
> Stablecoins also allow investment products (such as security and equity tokens) on crypto exchanges to be priced in fiat value rather than in cryptocurrency value. Tokens such as those designed to represent equity ownership, interest in funds, structured debt, loans, dividend rights, and other investment offerings benefit from stable price-pegging for both price and investment return.
>
> Finally and most simply, many exchanges do not offer any direct on- and off-ramp connectivity for fiat bank accounts. On these exchanges, stablecoins pegged to fiat reserves can provide the

---

15 White paper available at: https://f.hubspotusercontent30.net/hubfs/9304636/PDF/centre-whitepaper.pdf.

> needed integration for basic trading activity across multiple token types. Stablecoin gateways, created and maintained by licensed and compliant network members, become third-party fiat service providers for fiat connectivity to these exchanges.
>
> CENTRE provides the smart contracts and the governance that enables issuing network members to mint such stablecoins for customers who may then use them to manage risk exposure on supporting crypto asset exchanges and to invest in tokens that represent investment products.'

From USDC's launch in 2018 onwards its mantra has been 'digital money for the digital age'. The extract above from its white paper sets out some of its crypto exchange use cases. Its goal from the point of launch was to establish a financial ecosystem where USDC is accepted by as many wallets, exchanges, and service providers as possible.

The CENTRE Consortium has two founding members: the peer-to-peer payment services company Circle, and the cryptocurrency exchange, Coinbase. Circle's co-founders Jeremy Allaire and Sean Neville set out their vision for the future on Circle's blog in a post on 26 September 2018:

> 'We believe that an open internet of value exchange can transform and integrate the world more deeply, eventually eliminating artificial economic borders and enabling a more efficient and inclusive global marketplace that connects every person on the planet. The future of the global economy is open, shared, inclusive, far more evenly distributed, and powerful not only for a few chosen gatekeepers, but for all who will connect.
>
> This vision relies upon an open standards model for fiat money on the internet, which is emerging now with broad industry support behind USDC. The potential is immense, and we are excited to be part of this next step.'[16]

**USD Coin (USDC) unique features**

One of USDC's promoted points of difference as against other players in the stablecoin market concerns transparency. It purports to provide customers with an assurance that, for example, 1 USDC will allow them to withdraw US$1 should they wish to. The CENTRE Consortium has said that a major accounting firm is engaged to verify its cash reserves to ensure that it aligns with the number of issued tokens. USDC also benefits from the fact that its backers, Circle and Coinbase, are themselves established and well-funded.

USDC is seen as challenger to USDT's position in the stablecoin market. According to *coin-marketcap.com*, although USDT commanded a 74%/16% lead in market share in February 2021, this has shrunk to a 45%:30% lead in February 2022.

16 https://www.circle.com/blog/introducing-usd-coin.

**USD Coins in circulation**

Theoretically the number of USDC that can be in circulation is unlimited, save for the fact that every new coin that is created is backed by an equivalent US dollar reserve.

**How Is the USD Coin Network Secured?**

USDCs in circulation are ERC-20 tokens, which exist on the Ethereum blockchain.

**Where is USD Coin acquired?**

Given its backing, USDC is most closely associated with Coinbase. However, it can also be acquired on Poloniex, Binance, OKEx and Bitfinex, as well as decentralised exchanges such as Uniswap.

**5. Binance (BNB)**

| | |
|---|---|
| **Price** | US$293.50 |
| **Market dominance** | 3.75% |
| **Market rank** | 5 |
| **Market cap** | US$47,836,146,385.06 |
| **Fully diluted market cap** | US$48,375,158,346.03 |
| **All-time high** | US690.93 |
| **All-time low** | US$0.09611 |
| **Circulating supply** | 163,276,975 BNB |
| **Max supply** | 165,116,760 BNB |

**What Is BNB?**

BNB is associated with Binance, the largest cryptocurrency exchange globally based on daily trading volume. Binance supports various functionalities including: the Binance Chain, Binance Smart Chain, Binance Academy, Trust Wallet and Research projects, all of which exploit the potential of blockchain technology. BNB plays a role in many of the Binance sub-projects. Binance was founded by its CEO, Changpeng Zhao in 2017.

BNB is the native token of BNB Chain (former Binance Smart Chain and Binance Chain).[17] First minted in July 2017 on Ethereum, BNB is a utility token that allows holders to pay discounted fees for trading on Binance's exchange.

All transactions on BNB Smart Chain and BNB Beacon Chain are payable in either BEP-20 or BEP-2 BNB. Apart from trading fee discounts and enabling transactions, BNB can be

17 Description from https://www.binance.com/en/buy-BNB.

used for travel expenses and can be spent on products and services using the Binance Visa card. Holders can also donate BNB to charity via the Binance Charity Foundation (BCF) project.

**BNB's unique features**

Binance describes itself as a unique ecosystem of decentralised, blockchain-based networks. It is one of the leading crypto exchanges globally. Binance's main drive has been in the field of development; its stated mission is to become the infrastructure services provider for the entire blockchain ecosystem. The BNB token has also seen increased investor interest since 2021. Measures like BEP-95 have upgraded the deflationary tokenomics with the intention of making BNB more deflationary. The proposal was modelled on Ethereum's EIP-1559.

**BNB in circulation**

The initial maximum supply of BNB is 200,000,000 coins. As of September 2021, 168,137,036 were in circulation. At the time of writing, this figure stands at 163,276,975.

According to *coinmarketcap.com*:

> 'Binance conducts quarterly burning of the BNB supply, with the goal of reducing the total supply by half – or 100,000,000 BNB. On July 18, 2021, it conducted its 16th quarterly burning, which was worth $390 million in BNB price at the time of burning. However, that was not the most expensive burn – on April 16, 2021, the exchange burned nearly $600 million worth, in BNB price at the time of burning.'

According to the Binance white paper, exactly half of the maximum supply of BNB tokens was allocated towards the initial coin offering (ICO) and public sale of the token. The ICO was held in July 2017 shortly after the exchange launched, and saw Binance raise $15 million in funding, with BNB price at US$0.10 during the ICO. Taking BNB price today, that represents an almost 4200X return on investment (ROI). Another 40% of the total supply, or around 80,000,000 BNB coins, was distributed among the founding members and team. Finally, the remaining 10% of the maximum supply was split among angel investors.

**How Is the BNB Network Secured?**

BNB originated as an ERC-20 token on the Ethereum blockchain before being introduced on the company's own blockchain from where the coins were then issued, secured by the Tendermint byzantine-fault-tolerant (BFT) consensus mechanism.

Unlike a proof of stake consensus mechanism, the Binance blockchain does not support smart contract functionalities.

**How is BNB acquired?**

The easiest way to acquire BNB is through the associated Binance exchange, which supports the largest variety of trading pairs with BNB and the best trading rates for the coin.

### 6. Cardano (ADA)

| | |
|---|---|
| **Price** | US$0.6093 |
| **Market dominance** | 1.60% |
| **Market rank** | 6 |
| **Market cap** | US$20,423,005,290.03 |
| **Fully diluted market cap** | US$27,239,528,773.69 |
| **All-time high** | US$3.10 |
| **All-time low** | US$0.01735 |
| **Circulating supply** | 33,739,028,516 ADA |
| **Max supply** | 45,000,000,000 ADA |

**What Is Cardano (ADA)?**

Cardano is a decentralised third-generation proof-of-stake blockchain platform and home to the ADA cryptocurrency. According to Cardano's white paper:[18]

> 'It is the first blockchain platform to evolve out of a scientific philosophy and a research-first driven approach.
>
> The Cardano platform has been designed from the ground up and verified by an industry-leading combination of top engineers and academic experts in the fields of blockchain and cryptography. It has a strong focus on sustainability, scalability, and transparency. It is a fully open source project that aims to deliver an inclusive, fair, and resilient infrastructure for financial and social applications on a global scale. One of its primary goals is to bring reliable, secure financial services to those people who do not currently have access.
>
> Cardano has been designed with security as one of its founding principles. It is written in Haskell, a functional programming language. In a functional language like Haskell, building your system using pure functions is encouraged, which leads to a design where components are conveniently testable in isolation. Furthermore, advanced features of Haskell enable us to employ a whole range of powerful methods for ensuring correctness of the code, such as basing the implementation on formal and executable specifications, extensive property-based testing, and running tests in simulation.
>
> Cardano is developing a smart contract platform which seeks to deliver more advanced features than any protocol previously developed and will serve as a stable and secure platform for the

[18] https://docs.cardano.org/introduction.

> development of enterprise-level dApps. In the near future, Cardano will use a democratic governance system that allows the project to evolve over time, and fund itself in a sustainable way through a visionary treasury system.'

The open-source project also aims to 'redistribute power from unaccountable structures to the margins to individuals'.

Cardano was founded in 2017 by Charles Hoskinson, one of the co-founders of the Ethereum network. According to *coinmarketcap.com*, in August 2021, Charles Hoskinson announced the launch of the Alonzo hard fork, causing Cardano price to surge, gaining 116% in the following month. On 12 September 2021, the Cardano 'Alonzo' hard fork officially launched, bringing smart contract functionality to the blockchain. Over 100 smart contracts were launched within 24 hours. The ADA token is designed to ensure that owners can participate in the operation of the network: holders of the cryptocurrency can vote on any proposed amendments to the software.

**Cardano's unique features**

Cardano is among the largest blockchains to employ a proof-of-stake consensus mechanism.

According to the Cardano team, it boasts the following advantages:[19]

> 'Academic research — formal methods, such as mathematical specifications, property-based tests, and proofs, are the best way to deliver high assurance software systems and give confidence to users for the management of digital funds. Cardano has been built using formal methods to achieve strong guarantees on the functional correctness of core components of the system. All of the research and technical specifications that underpin Cardano are publicly available, and all Cardano development activity is published online.
>
> System design — Cardano is written in Haskell, a secure functional programming language that encourages building a system using pure functions, which leads to a design where components are conveniently testable in isolation. Furthermore, advanced features of Haskell enable us to employ a whole range of powerful methods for ensuring correctness of the code, such as basing the implementation on formal and executable specifications, extensive property-based testing, and running tests in simulation.
>
> Security — Ouroboros (the Cardano proof-of-stake protocol) establishes rigorous security guarantees; it was delivered with several peer-reviewed papers presented in top-tier conferences and publications in the area of cybersecurity and cryptography.
>
> Power consumption — Cardano is a proof-of-stake blockchain. In contrast to proof-of-work blockchains, Cardano requires much less energy and computational power. The Bitcoin network grows through computers doing ever-more-energy-intensive computations – proof of

19 https://docs.cardano.org/new-to-cardano/why-use-cardano.

work – which is unsustainable in the long term. Cambridge University has an online tool that shows the computers powering Bitcoin already consume twice as much energy as Switzerland every year.

Seamless upgrades — traditionally, blockchains upgrade using hard forks. When conducting a hard fork, the current protocol would stop operating, new rules and changes would be implemented, and the chain would restart – with its previous history being erased. Cardano handles hard forks differently. Instead of implementing radical changes, the Cardano hard-fork combinator technology ensures a smooth transition to a new protocol while saving the history of the previous blocks and not causing any disruptions for end users.

Decentralization — Cardano is maintained by almost 3,000 distributed stake pools that are operated by the community. All blocks and transactions are validated by network participants without any reliance on a centralized authority.

Functional environment for business use cases — Cardano is establishing a foundation for global, decentralized finance to develop a range of DApps that can run using functional and domain-specific smart contracts, providing multi-asset tokens for any needs.'

The project advertises the fact that all of the technology goes through a peer-reviewed research phase. According to *coinmarketcap.com*,

'in 2020, Cardano held a Shelley upgrade that aimed to make its blockchain "50 to 100 times more decentralized" than other large blockchains. At the time, Hoskinson predicted that this would pave the way for hundreds of assets to run on its network. The Alonzo hard fork launch in September 2021 will bring an end to the Shelley era, and usher in the Goguen phase. Users can develop and deploy smart contracts on Cardano, allowing native decentralized applications (DApps) to be built on blockchain. Cardano price broke the $3 mark and hit an all-time high of $3.101 on Sept. 2, 2021, ahead of the launch.'

**Cardano in circulation**

There is a maximum supply of 45 billion ADA.

At the time of writing, there is a circulating supply of 33,752,565,071 ADA. Five rounds of public sales of Cardano tokens were held between September 2015 and January 2017.

Cardano is secured through what it describes as an 'environmentally sustainable, verifiably secure' proof of stake protocol known as Ouroboros. Cardano says that Ouroboros improves upon the security guarantees that are delivered by a proof of work consensus mechanism while using substantially less power, purportedly four times more energy-efficient than Bitcoin.

In February 2022, the number of Cardano wallets broke the three million milestone. Since December 2020, it has surged by 1,200%, from 190,000 to over 3,000,000, coinciding with an increase in smart contracts following the Alonzo Upgrade. Cardano reached the 1,000 smart contracts milestone on 27 January 2022.

**How is Cardano (ADA) acquired?**

Cardano is available on all major exchanges, including Binance, Bittrex, eToro, and HitBTC.

**7. XRP**

| | |
|---|---|
| **Price** | US$0.3919 |
| **Market dominance** | 1.56% |
| **Market rank** | 7 |
| **Market cap** | US$18,956,594,064.70 |
| **Fully diluted market cap** | US$39,212,614,820.57 |
| **All-time high** | US$3.87 |
| **All-time low** | US$0.002802 |
| **Circulating supply** | 48,343,101,197 XRP |
| **Max supply** | 100,000,000,000 XRP |

**What Is XRP?**

XRP is the native cryptocurrency of products developed by Ripple Labs Inc. XRP is its 'digital asset built for global payments'.

Ripple was founded in 2012 by Chris Larsen and Jed McCaleb and is based on the work of Ryan Fugger, who created the XRP Ledger in 2012. The XRP Ledger is an open-source cryptographic ledger powered by a peer-to-peer network of nodes. Following a rebrand from OpenCoin to Ripple, the enterprise pursued partnerships with Bank of America, Santander and Standard Chartered.

**How Does XRP Work?**

Ripple purports to be a cheaper and more efficient alternative to the SWIFT payment system used to process international transactions. This is supposed to happen via the Internet of Value, the umbrella term for several of Ripple's products: RippleNet, the XRP Ledger, the XRP coin and RippleX.

RippleNet is its global network that financial institutions are able to use to transfer money more quickly and at a lower cost than through traditional systems. This is apparently possible because of the single API needed to connect to RippleNet. XRP Ledger is Ripple's open-source blockchain with the XRP coin as its native asset. It runs independently of the Ripple company, although Ripple uses it for various purposes. While not as popular as other blockchains, the XRP Ledger can also be used as a settlement layer.

In contrast to Ethereum, the XRP Ledger does not use a proof-of-work consensus mechanism. It also does not work with a proof-of-stake consensus mechanism like many other cryptocurrencies. Instead, it uses the XRP Ledger Consensus Protocol, which professedly reduces transaction finality time and transaction costs.

RippleX is a platform offering blockchain solutions to projects that want to provide payment-oriented services. Instead of building their own DApps and blockchain solutions, companies can use RippleX and the XRP Ledger to provide mainstream compatibility. Ripple is considered by some to be an attractive proposition for cross-border payments.

**How is XRP acquired?**

XRP is available on most centralised exchanges, including Binance, Huobi Global, Bybit, FTX, Bitfinex, Kraken and others.

**8. Binance USD**

| | |
|---|---|
| **Price** | US$1.00 |
| **Market dominance** | 1.50% |
| **Market rank** | 8 |
| **Market cap** | US$18,276,014,759.65 |
| **Fully diluted market cap** | US$18,276,014,759.65 |
| **All-time high** | US$1.11 |
| **All-time low** | US$0.8861 |
| **Circulating supply** | 18,279,534,109 BUSD |
| **Max supply** | – |

**What is BUSD?**

Binance USD (BUSD) is a 1:1 USD-backed stablecoin approved by the New York State Department of Financial Services, issued by Binance (in partnership with Paxos).

The BUSD Monthly Audit Report can be viewed from the official website.

Launched on 5 September 2019, BUSD is a digital fiat currency, issued as ERC-20 and supports BEP-2. The stablecoin grew from a market capitalisation of approximately US$1 billion at the start of 2021, to over US$14.6 billion at the end of 2021. It is the third largest stablecoin by market cap, behind Tether and USDC. The expansion of its use is apparently due to increased user adoption as wallets, platforms and services, DEXes and CEXes support BUSD.

According to coinmarketcap.com:

> 'Top wallets like Metamask, Trust Wallet, Trezor, Zapper and many more allow users to hold BUSD now. Platforms and services, like travel booking site Travala, payments gateways like Moonpay and Banxa, payment APIs like Wyre and multi-currency payment services like

ivendPay and Paylot are now supporting BUSD too. While PancakeSwap is the top DEX in the BSC ecosystem, numerous other top DEXes also support BUSD, including: Uniswap, 1inch, Curve Finance, Ellipsis, MDEX, SushiSwap, 0x and many more. Users of centralized exchanges (CEXes) can use BUSD outside of Binance and Binance.US too, with top exchanges like FTX, Gate.io, WazirX, MEXC and more. For users interested in yield farming and lending BUSD, it is available on centralized platforms like Binance, Blockfi and Celsius, among others. Top DeFi protocols like Venus, Aave, yearn.finance and more also allow users to earn yield on their BUSD.'

**How is BUSD acquired?**

BUSD is available from most major exchanges.

**9. Solana**

| | |
|---|---|
| **Price** | US$39.37 |
| **Market dominance** | 1.10% |
| **Market rank** | 9 |
| **Market cap** | US$13,391,824,355.46 |
| **Fully diluted market cap** | US$20,125,676,815.66 |
| **All-time high** | US$260.06 |
| **All-time low** | US$0.5052 |
| **Circulating supply** | 340,434,975 SOL |
| **Total supply** | 511,616,946 SOL |
| **Max supply** | – |

**What Is Solana (SOL)?**

Solana is a decentralised computing platform that uses SOL to pay for transactions.

Solana's stated aims are to improve blockchain scalability by using a combination of proof of stake consensus along with so-called 'proof of history'. Solana claims to be able to support 50,000 transactions per second without sacrificing decentralisation. More specifically, Solana is a crypto-computing platform that aims to achieve high transaction speeds without sacrificing decentralisation. Like Ethereum, Solana is both a cryptocurrency and a platform for running decentralised apps (dapps), ranging from Degenerate Apes to the Serum decentralised exchange (or DEX). Its particular boast is speed, which is achieved via an assortment of technologies including a consensus mechanism called 'proof of history' (PoH). Solana can apparently process around 50,000 transactions per second – compared to 15 or less for Ethereum.[20] As a result of its speed, congestion and usage fees

20 https://www.coinbase.com/price/solana.

are comparatively low. It is the hope of Solana's developers that it will come to compete with payment processors such as Visa.

Solana's native cryptocurrency is SOL, which is used to pay transaction fees and for staking. It also gives holders the right to vote in future upgrades.

Solana was officially launched in March 2020 by the Solana Foundation with headquarters in Geneva, Switzerland. Because of the innovative hybrid consensus model, Solana enjoys interest from both smaller and institutional traders.

**Solana's unique features**

Solana's key innovation is the proof-of-history consensus developed by Anatoly Yakovenko. This concept allows for greater scalability of the protocol, which in turn boosts usability. This 'new blockchain architecture based on proof-of-history' is described in the following terms in Solana's white paper:[21]

> 'A proof for verifying order and passage of time between events. PoH is used to encode trustless passage of time into a ledger – an append only data structure. When used alongside a consensus algorithm such as Proof of Work (PoW) or Proof of Stake (PoS), PoH can reduce messaging overhead in a Byzantine Fault Tolerant replicated state machine, resulting inn sub-second finality times. This paper also proposes two algorithms that leverage the time keeping properties of the PoH ledger – a PoS algorithm that can recover from partitions of any size and an efficient streaming Proof of Replication (PoRep). The combination of PoRep and PoH provides a defense against forgery of the ledger with respect to time (ordering) and storage. The protocol is analyzed on a 1 gbps network, and this paper shows that throughput up to 710k transactions per second is possible with todays hardware.
>
> [...]
>
> Proof of History is a sequence of computation that can provide a way to cryptographically verify passage of time between two events. It uses a cryptographically secure function written so that output cannot be predicted from the input, and must be completely executed to generate the output. The function is run in a sequence on a single core, its previous output as the current input, periodically recording the current output, and how many times its been called. The output can then be re-computed and verified by external computers in parallel by checking each sequence segment on a separate core. Data can be timestamped into this sequence by appending the data (or a hash of some data) into the state of the function. The recording of the state, index and data as it was appended into the sequences provides a timestamp that can guarantee that the data was created sometime before the next hash was generated in the sequence. This design also supports horizontal scaling as multiple generators can synchronize amongst each other by mixing their state into each others sequences.'

21 White paper available at https://solana.com/solana-whitepaper.pdf.

It follows that Solana's reputation is based in part on short processing times. The hybrid protocol allows for faster validation for both transaction and smart contract execution.

As described by *coinmarketcap.com*, Solana recently experienced a noteworthy bull run, where its price gained over 700% since mid-July 2021. 'The launch of the Degenerate Ape NFT collection sent SOL price to an all-time high (ATH) above $60, and it has been climbing since, largely due to developer activity on the Solana ecosystem, greater institutional interest, growing DeFi ecosystem, and the rise of the NFTs and gaming vertical on Solana. Solana price rose to an ATH of $216 on Sept. 9, 2021.'[22]

**Solana (SOL) in circulation**

The current circulating supply of Solana is 340,434,890 SOL out of a total supply of 511,616,946 SOL.

As indicated above, Solana employs a specific combination of proof-of-history and proof-of-stake consensus mechanisms. The former is responsible for the majority of transaction processing. It records successful operations and the time passing between them. The proof-of-stake mechanism is a monitoring tool for the proof-of-history mechanism; it validates the blocks produced by it.

**How is Solana (SOL) acquired?**

SOL is available on most exchanges, including Binance, Coinbase, FTX and Bilaxy.

**10. Dogecoin**

| | |
|---|---|
| **Price** | US$0.08019 |
| **Market dominance** | 0.87% |
| **Market rank** | 10 |
| **Market cap** | US$10,623,486,770.56 |
| **Fully diluted market cap** | US$10,623,486,770.56 |
| **All-time high** | US$0.7376 |
| **All-time low** | US$0.00008547 |
| **Circulating supply** | 132,670,764,300 DOGE |
| **Total supply** | 132,670,764,300 DOGE |
| **Max supply** | – |

**What Is Dogecoin?**

Dogecoin is a community-driven cryptocurrency that was inspired by a Shiba Inu meme.

22 https://coinmarketcap.com/currencies/solana/.

The Dogecoin Core software allows anyone to operate a node in the Dogecoin blockchain networks and uses the Scrypt hashing method for proof-of-work. It is adapted from Bitcoin Core and other cryptocurrencies.[23]

The open-source digital currency was created by Billy Markus from Portland, Oregon and Jackson Palmer from Sydney, Australia. It was forked from Litecoin in December 2013. The cryptocurrency was originally envisaged as a playful, light-hearted cryptocurrency that would have popular appeal given that it was based on an amusing dog meme.

Dogecoin is different from the proof-of-work protocol used by Bitcoin in that it utilises Scrypt technology. Its total supply is uncapped, and it has a block time of 1 minute. As with Bitcoin, Dogecoins can be mined as a solo endeavour or prospective miners can join a mining pool. Dogecoin is used as a tipping system on social media platforms Reddit and Twitter to reward quality content.

[23] A copy of Dogecoin's white paper is available at: https://github.com/dogecoin/dogecoin/blob/master/README.md.

*Chapter 5*

# Regulation of cryptocurrency in the United Kingdom



## A. INTRODUCTION

**5.01** This chapter provides an overview of the current state of regulation of cryptocurrency in the UK. It reflects the position as of April 2022.

As has been indicated in previous chapters in this work, there is no blanket prohibition on cryptocurrencies in the UK. While certain aspects of the UK anti-money laundering ('AML') regime applies specifically to cryptoasset activities, the UK does not (yet) have a standalone regulatory regime for cryptoassets. As such, the question of whether a specific cryptocurrency is going to be subject to financial regulation in the UK will ultimately depend on whether it is within the scope of the Financial Conduct Authority's ('FCA') regulatory perimeter. Cryptocurrencies may also fall within the payment services and electronic money regime established under the Payment Services Regulations 2017 ('PSRs') and the Electronic Money Regulations 2011 ('EMRs'). Passing reference will be made to the FCA's AML and counter-terrorist financing regime in relation to cryptoasset exchange providers and wallet providers under the Money Laundering, Terrorist Financing and Transfer of Funds (Information on the Payer) Regulations 2017 (SI 2017/692) ('MLRs'), which came into force on 10 January 2020, but which falls outside of the scope of this work.

The content of this chapter is chiefly based on the FCA's guidance on cryptoassets which is appended to the *FCA Policy Statement: Guidance on Cryptoassets: Feedback and Final Guidance to CP19/3 (July 2019) (PS19/22)*.

It is important to state that this chapter proceeds on the basis that any given cryptoasset in question is covered by UK jurisdiction. One of the most common issues for practitioners concerns whether the UK regulators have authority over token issuers, promotors, or others in involved in the process. In a nutshell, the position is that the location of the cryptoasset is deemed to be where the owner of it is domiciled. It is upon this assumption that the material set out in this chapter is based.

## B. THE FCA REGULATORY PERIMETER

**5.02** The FCA's aim and purpose is set out in the Financial Services and Markets Act 2000 ('FSMA 2000'). Its strategic goal is to ensure that the relevant financial markets function well. This is underpinned by three statutory 'operational objectives': to secure an appropriate degree of protection for consumers; to protect and enhance the integrity of the UK's financial system; and to promote effective competition in the interest of consumers.

The 'regulatory perimeter' refers to the conceptual boundary between regulated and unregulated financial services activities.

Activities that fall within the FCA's perimeter are regulated and require authorisation from the FCA (or the Prudential Regulatory Authority if they concern certain deposit-taking/insurance activities) before a firm can carry them out. The perimeter includes specified activities and investments set out in FSMA 2000 and the Financial Services and Markets Act 2000 (Regulated Activities) Order 2001 ('RAO'). Regulated activities are often defined under EU law, which is then transposed into domestic law or applied directly. The Markets in Financial Instruments Directive ('MiFID II') recognises various 'Financial Instruments'. These are certain categories of investments to which MiFID applies, which have been mapped to the RAO.

For example, providing advice in relation to a specified investment like a share may amount to the regulated activity of 'advising on investments' which would likely require authorisation. By contrast, providing advice in relation to something other than a specified investment, such as a commodity, like gold, is not within the regulatory perimeter, and is not a regulated activity, and so would not require authorisation.

As set out in the FCA's guidance, activities can also fall within the FCA perimeter by virtue of other legislation. For example, providing payment services is regulated under the PSRs. Issuing e-money is regulated under the EMRs, but it is also a regulated activity under FSMA when it is carried on by credit institutions, credit unions and municipal banks. Market participants that carry on regulated activities involving e-money tokens need to ensure they have the correct permissions and follow the relevant rules and regulations.[1]

1 *FCA Policy Statement: Guidance on Cryptoassets: Feedback and Final Guidance to CP19/3* (July 2019) (PS19/22), at 29.

The FCA recognises that people may purchase cryptoassets for speculative reasons and in anticipation of an increase in value. However, the fact that a cryptoasset is acquired for value does not necessarily make it a specified investment under the RAO, nor a financial instrument under MiFID.

## C. FINANCIAL REGULATION BY CATEGORY: SECURITY TOKENS, E-MONEY TOKENS, EXCHANGE TOKENS, UTILITY TOKENS, STABLECOINS

**5.03** As explained in Chapter 2, there is no universally accepted definition or taxonomy to categorise cryptoassets.

A cryptoasset can be described as a cryptographically secured digital representation of value or contractual rights that uses some form of DLT and can be transferred, stored or traded electronically. The UK Cryptoassets Taskforce (comprising the FCA, the Bank of England, HM Treasury) has categorised cryptoassets into varieties of token based on their essential characteristics: *security tokens*, *exchange tokens*, and *utility tokens*.

That said, cryptoassets are generally used as follows.

1. As a means of exchange, functioning as a decentralised tool to enable the buying and selling of goods and services, or to facilitate regulated payment services.
2. For investment, with firms and consumers gaining direct exposure by holding and trading cryptoassets, or indirect exposure by holding and trading financial instruments that reference cryptoassets.
3. To support capital raising and/or the creation of decentralised networks through Initial Coin Offerings (ICOs).[2]

The 'taxonomy' set out in the FCA Guidance broadly adopts the definitions set out in the UK Cryptoassets Taskforce Report, subject to certain refinements.

The FCA Guidance taxonomy divides cryptoassets into regulated and unregulated cryptoassets. The UK Cryptoassets Taskforce definitions of exchange tokens and utility tokens are retained, and together comprise 'unregulated tokens'. Cryptoassets that are deemed to constitute electronic money are divided from the Taskforce category of security token and are instead categorised as 'e-money tokens,' and the two sub-categories of cryptoassets (security tokens other than e-money tokens, and e-money tokens) comprise 'regulated tokens' for FCA purposes.

Each are discussed in detail below, starting with regulated tokens.

---

2 *Cryptoassets Taskforce: Final Report (30 October 2018)*, at 2.12.

As suggested above, regulated tokens are tokens that are regulated either under FSMA or the EMRs. Security tokens (ie tokens that are specified investments, excluding e-money tokens) are within the FSMA perimeter. E-money tokens are within the FSMA perimeter if issued by a credit institution, a credit union, or a municipal bank, and are also regulated under the EMRs.

## i. Security tokens[3]

**5.04** A security token is a category of token that falls within the FCA's regulatory perimeter.

A security token provides rights and obligations akin to specified investments as set out in the RAO (excluding e-money). Such tokens can also be classified as financial instruments under MiFID II.

By way of example, these tokens have characteristics that are identical or similar to traditional instruments, for example, shares and debentures, or indeed rights to such instruments. The FCA considers a security to broadly refer to an instrument that indicates an ownership position in an entity, a creditor relationship with an entity, or rights to ownership or profit. Security tokens include tokens that grant holders some or all of the rights conferred on shareholders or debt-holders, as well as those tokens that give rights to other tokens that are in themselves specified investments.

A full list of specified investments is contained in the RAO.

The FCA's Guidance contains explanatory narrative on some of the specified investments that are likely to be most relevant in the security market context. Some of these are summarised below.

*1. Shares*

**5.05** Under Article 76 of the RAO, the specified investment category of shares etc includes shares or stock in the capital of any body corporate (including those that are not incorporated), and any unincorporated body constituted under the law of a country or territory outside of the UK. Shares can also be transferable securities under MiFID.

The FCA considers that all shares (and securitised debt) that are negotiable on the capital markets will fall within the definition of transferable securities. It does not consider that the shares must

3 *FCA Policy Statement: Guidance on Cryptoassets: Feedback and Final Guidance to CP19/3 (July 2019) (PS19/22)*, at paras 64–67. The following narrative is derived from para 68 of the FCA Guidance.

be listed in order to be a transferable security under MIFID. The focus on 'negotiability' means that the tokens must be capable of being traded on the capital markets.

Factors that have been taken to indicate that a token is negotiable on the capital markets include whether it can be transferred from one person to another meaning ownership of the token is transferred, and, whether it gives the person who acquires it good legal title to the token. The matter of whether a particular form of overseas body constitutes a body corporate will depend on whether the law under which it is established confers on it the status of incorporation. The FCA considers that separate legal personality is a significant factor but not determinative. Another significant factor is that the body survives a change of member. The definition also applies to overseas unincorporated bodies, but these bodies must have a share capital.

As such, tokens that bestow similar rights to shares, like voting rights, or access to a dividend of company profits or the distribution of capital upon liquidation, are likely to be deemed to be security tokens. The same applies to tokens that represent ownership or control, given that shares typically represent ownership (through capital distribution and dividends) and control by means of voting. However, this will not always be the case as some tokens will provide voting rights without giving rise to control (eg a token that provides the holder with the right to vote on future ICOs the firm in question will invest in but no other rights may not constitute a share as those rights do not provide control-like decisions on the future of the business). The voting rights that are typically associated with being a shareholder are specific and fall within the remit of company law. This means that the question of whether the token is equivalent to a share depends on the operation of the specific firm and corporate law.

In order for a token to be considered a transferable security for MIFID purposes, it must be negotiable (ie capable of being traded) on the capital markets.

Note that even if a token which acts like a share is not a transferable security under MiFID, it may still constitute a specified investment (and therefore may be a security token).

*2. Debt instruments*

**5.06** Article 77 (debentures) includes debentures, loan stock, bonds, debenture stock, certificates of deposit, and any other instruments that create or acknowledge indebtedness (subject to certain exclusions). With the exception of government and public securities, all forms of debt securities that are negotiable on the capital markets also fall within the definition of transferable securities under MiFID. Debt securities do not need to be listed. This category also includes some money market instruments. Accordingly, a token that creates or acknowledges indebtedness by representing money owed to the token holder is considered a debenture and will constitute a security token.

*3. Warrants*

**5.07** The specified investment category of warrants is provided in Article 79 of the RAO.

Warrants are one of many categories of specified investments that are expressed in terms of the rights that they bestow in relation to other categories of specified investment. The rights conferred must be rights to 'subscribe' for the relevant investments. This will mean that they are rights to acquire the investments directly from the issuer of the investments and by way of the issue of new investments rather than by purchasing investments that have already been issued. For example, if a firm issued A tokens that grant token holders the right to subscribe for B tokens in the future, and B tokens are themselves specified investments (for example, shares or debentures), A tokens will likely constitute warrants and will therefore be a security token.

*4. Certificates representing certain securities*

**5.08** Article 80 of the RAO encompasses certificates and other instruments that confer contractual or property rights over other investments, such as shares or debentures. This is subject to two conditions: (i) the investment must be owned by someone other than the individual on whom the certificates confer the rights; and (ii) the consent of that individual is not a prerequisite for the transfer of those investments. Depository receipts will fall within this category. In terms of application to tokens, a token may confer rights in relation to tokenised shares or tokenised debentures (including depositary receipts on the holder). These are likely to fall within the category of security tokens.

*5. Units in collective investment schemes*

**5.09** Article 81 of the RAO encompasses units in a collective investment scheme and includes units in a unit trust scheme or authorised contractual scheme, shares in open-ended investment companies and rights in respect of most limited partnerships and all limited partnership schemes. According to the FCA, a collective investment scheme means any arrangement, the purpose or effect of which is to enable persons taking part in the arrangements to participate in or receive profits or income arising from the investment or sums paid out of such profits or income. The participants do not have day-to-day control over the management of the investment and contributions of the participants, and profits from which payments are to be made, are pooled and/or the investment are managed as a whole by or on behalf of the operator of the scheme. Note that certain arrangements are excluded. Shares in, or securities of, an open-ended investment company are treated differently from shares in other companies (they are not captured by the specified investment category of shares). A token that acts as a vehicle through which profits or income are shared or pooled, or where the investment is managed as a whole by a market participant, for instance the issuer of tokens, is likely to constitute a collective investment scheme. Factors indicating that a token being such a security may include references to pooled investments, pooled contributions or pooled profits in a white paper.

*6. Rights and interests in investments*

**5.10** Rights to or interests in certain investments (including those identified above, from shares or units in a collective investment scheme) will also constitute a specified investment under the RAO in their own right. Tokens representing rights to or interests in other specified investments will therefore constitute securities. For example, a firm may issue a token that represents a right in a share (although the token itself may not represent or have the characteristics of a share). This type of token will be designated a security token by the FCA.

## ii. E-money tokens[4]

**5.11** E-money is electronically stored monetary value as represented by a claim on the electronic money issuer which is: issued on receipt of funds for the purpose of making payment transactions; accepted by a person other than the electronic money issuer; and not excluded by regulation 3 of the EMRs. E-money must enable users to make payment transactions with third parties, so it must be accepted by more parties than just the issuer. E-money includes fiat balances in various types of online wallets or prepaid cards.

E-money tokens are tokens that fall within the definition of e-money under the EMRs. Firms issuing e-money must ensure they are appropriately authorised or registered. The issuance of e-money is regulated under the EMRs and is a regulated activity under Article 9B of the RAO when carried on by credit institutions, credit unions, and municipal banks.

Electronic storage of monetary value includes the possibility of using DLT and cryptographically secured tokens to represent fiat funds. Cryptoassets that establish a new sort of unit of account rather than representing fiat funds are unlikely to amount to e-money unless the value of the unit is pegged to a fiat currency, but even then, it will still depend on the facts of each case. Within the sandbox many firms have facilitated DLT-based e-money to provide more efficient, automated, and transparent services, including for international payments. According to the FCA, some tokens might be stabilised by being pegged to a fiat currency, most commonly the USD, and most commonly with a 1:1 backing. This is a form of 'stablecoin' known as a 'fiat backed', 'fiat collateralised' or 'deposit backed' stablecoin. This stablecoin looks to hold a consistent value with the fiat currency and is theoretically 'backed' by fiat currency.

Any token that is pegged to a currency, like USD or GBP, or other assets, and is used for the payment of goods or services on a network could potentially meet the definition of e-money (subject to also meeting the aforementioned requirements).

4 Ibid, at paras 69–74.

*It is important to stress that descriptions given in issuing documents, usually 'white papers', will often describe labels to tokens which may not be accurate.* Often a token described as a utility is far from that and in fact requires registration as a security token.

### iii. Exchange tokens[5]

**5.12** As indicated above, unregulated tokens are tokens that do not offer rights or obligations akin to specified investments. These tokens can be centrally issued, decentralised, primarily used as a means of exchange, or grant access to a current or prospective product or service. They might be used in one or many networks or ecosystems. Unregulated tokens can be 'privacy tokens', 'fungible utility tokens', 'non-fungible tokens', 'access tokens' etc. They can be fully transferable or have restricted transferability.

*As highlighted by the FCA, the key thing to note is that any token that is not a security token or an e-money token, is an unregulated token, but it is crucial to remember the caution as to mislabelling above.* The FCA's analysis of unregulated tokens is based on the categories explored by the UK Cryptoasset Taskforce, and a further category specific to the FCA's guidance: exchange tokens, utility tokens, and stablecoins.

Starting with the term 'exchange token', this is often used synonymously with 'cryptocurrency', though the latter is merely an example of the former.

*However, while exchange tokens can be used as a means of exchange, they are not currently recognised as legal tender in the UK, and they are not considered to be a currency or money.*

Security tokens are generally more volatile than any currencies and commodities in general circulation. The result is that they are not commonly accepted as a means of exchange in the UK (outside crypto and digital communities), and they are not typically used as a unit of account or a store of value. As explained in Chapter 2, exchange tokens usually do not bestow upon the token holder any of the rights associated with specified investments. The reason for this is that they are typically decentralised and have no issuer to honour any contractual rights.

As noted above, the FCA acknowledges that exchange tokens can be acquired and held with the intention of speculating (rather than for exchange), as token-holders may predict that the value of such tokens will increase, depending on the cryptoasset markets. The FCA does not see this as being sufficient reason to treat exchange tokens as specified investments.

5 Ibid, at paras 34–47.

*It follows that exchange tokens currently fall outside the regulatory perimeter. This means that the transferring, buying, and selling of these tokens, including the commercial operation of cryptoasset exchanges for exchange tokens, are activities not currently regulated by the FCA.* For example, an exchange facilitating transactions of cryptocurrencies such as Bitcoin between participants is not carrying on a regulated activity.

## iv. Utility tokens[6]

**5.13** Utility tokens provide consumers with access to a current or prospective service or product and often grant rights similar to pre-payment vouchers. They can sometimes have similarities to rewards-based crowdfunding. As is the case with exchange tokens, utility tokens can usually be traded on the secondary markets and be used for speculative investment purposes. This in and of itself does not mean that these tokens will constitute specified investments if they do not have the characteristics of relevant specified investments. Given that utility tokens do not have the features of security tokens, they will not be captured by the FCA's regulatory regime.

## v. Stablecoins[7]

**5.14** As explained by the FCA in its guidance, there is no single definition of a 'stablecoin'. It is a term associated with tokens that feature a variety of mechanisms to stabilise their value. Thus, stablecoins are a response to the volatility of cryptoassets. Stablecoins are therefore a type of token and, depending on what they are backed with and how they are structured, they can fall into many different categories of the FCA's taxonomy.

For example, a stablecoin could be considered a unit in a collective investment scheme, or a debt security, or other types of specified investment. On the other hand, a stablecoin could also be outside of the FCA's regulatory perimeter.

Whether a stablecoin is or is not regulated will fall to be assessed on a case-by-case basis.

The FCA notes that the most common methods of stabilisation are:

- *Fiat-backed stabilisation*: these tokens are backed with fiat currencies, most commonly the United States Dollar (USD), but some tokens are backed with the British Pound (GBP) or a collection of currencies. In some cases, this involves the issuer 'pegging' the value to that

6 Ibid, at paras 48–50.
7 Ibid, at paras 51–53.

currency, ie guaranteeing the value of the token, while holding a reserve of fiat currency to ensure it can meet any claims. Examples of such cryptocurrencies currently among the top 10 cryptocurrencies by market capitalisation are described in Chapter 4. In other examples, the token gives the token holder an interest or right to the custodied fiat currency, with the value of the tokens being directly linked to the value of the fiat currency held.

- *Crypto-collateralised stabilisation*: these tokens are backed with a basket of cryptoassets with the intention of spreading risk and insulating the holder from the impact of volatility.
- *Asset-backed stabilisation*: these tokens are backed with a tangible or intangible asset that usually has some economic value, eg gold.
- *Algorithmic stabilisation*: these tokens attempt stabilisation through algorithms that may, for example, control the supply of the tokens to influence price.

As noted by the FCA:

> 'Where attempts have been made to stabilise the volatility of cryptoassets these tokens will be regulated where they provide rights or obligations akin to specified investments as security tokens and e-money tokens do. If they do not, they will be unregulated tokens, but some of the activities performed may still be subject to regulation, for instance AML requirements.
>
> Tokens might be backed by financial assets, physical assets, or other cryptoassets. These tokens may in certain circumstances be security tokens or e-money tokens, depending on among other things, the rights granted by such tokens, the nature of the underlying assets and other relevant arrangements. For example, while gold itself is not a specified investment, a token that gives token holders a right or interest to gold held by a token issuer, or rights to payments from profit or income generated from the holding, buying or selling of gold may in certain circumstances be a specified investment. For example this could be a unit in a collective investment scheme or a debt security.
>
> Other arrangements might cause the token to meet the definition of e-money.'[8]

## vi. Summary of FCA approach

**5.15** In summary, the FCA's taxonomy divides cryptoassets into regulated and unregulated cryptoassets. The instruments that are regulated under FSMA are set out in an exhaustive manner in the RAO. These are 'specified investments' (including, eg instruments such as shares, bonds etc). As such, when assessing whether a cryptocurrency is subject to financial regulation it is necessary to analyse whether the specific asset meets the definition of a specified investment in the RAO. The tokens that do will qualify as security tokens in the FCA's Guidance and will typically be the subject of financial regulation in the UK. The key thing to note is that any token that is not a security token or an e-money token, is an unregulated token.

8 Ibid, at paras 54–56.

In practice this means that an assessment of whether a token is regulated will be conducted on a case-by-case basis.

The FCA has noted so-called 'dual tokens' (ie where tokens move between categories during their lifecycle, sometimes working in tandem with other tokens during the launch of a new network). In either case, the FCA has emphasised that 'the regulatory treatment depends on the token's intrinsic structure, the rights attached to the tokens and how they are used in practice. If a token at a point in time reaches the definition of an e-money token or a security token, then it will fall under regulation'.[9] The analysis will focus less on extrinsic factors, such as the intended use of the relevant cryptocurrency or contextual factors (such as whether a related platform is currently operational or whether the underlying network is decentralised).

In a matrimonial finance context, the tokens encountered are more likely to be exchange tokens than those falling into the other categories. 'Classic' cryptocurrencies such as Bitcoin, Litecoin etc, which are not centrally issued and confer no rights or entitlements on the holders fall into the category of 'exchange token' and are not therefore currently regulated by the FCA.

Activities related to cryptocurrencies such as Bitcoin are at present unlikely to trigger licensing requirements in the UK, although registration under the extended UK anti-money laundering regime may be required.

## D. AML/CTF FINANCING

**5.16** The application of the UK anti-money laundering and counter-terrorist financing ('CTF') regime to cryptoassets is beyond the scope of this work. However, by way of summary, the UK AML requirements are principally contained in the MLRs. The MLRs implement the Fourth EU Money Laundering Directive in the UK and provide for various requirements on business that fall within its scope, including the requirement to perform a firm-level AML risk assessment, organisational requirements concerning AML (eg record keeping), customer due diligence, and ongoing monitoring obligations. The MLRs only apply to certain businesses.

Since 10 January 2020, existing businesses (operating immediately before 10 January 2020) carrying on cryptoasset activity in the UK have needed to be compliant with the MLRs including the requirement to be registered with the FCA by 9 January 2021 in order to continue to carry on business. A new cryptoasset business that intends to begin to trade in the UK must be registered with the FCA before commencement of business. The change from 10 January 2020 brought cryptoasset exchange providers and custodian wallet providers within the scope of the MLRs.

9 Ibid, at para 4.6.

As such, the MLRs impact anybody conducting cryptoasset business of a kind that falls within the definitions of 'cryptoasset exchange provider' or 'custodian wallet provider' in the UK. This includes existing UK authorised financial services firms if they carry on relevant cryptoasset business.

## E. REGULATORY DEVELOPMENTS IN THE UK

**5.17** The first quarter of 2022 saw various announcements from the UK government concerning the regulation of cryptoassets in the UK.

On 4 April 2022, John Glen, Economic Secretary to the Treasury gave a keynote speech which outlined the UK government's plans to make the UK a 'world-leading regime' for cryptoassets. Rishi Sunak, former Chancellor of the Exchequer, announced a similar intention of making the UK a 'global hub for cryptoasset technology'. He also raised the prospect of commissioning the Royal Mint to produce an NFT. At the heart of the plans announced by the UK government was the intention to see stablecoins recognised as a valid form of payment.

The announcement covered the following points:[10]

- Stablecoins are to be brought within the regulatory perimeter, paving their way for use in the UK as a recognised form of payment.
- This will fall among a series of measures designed to establish the UK as a 'global hub' for cryptoasset technology and investment.
- Further measures were announced that will provide for a 'financial market infrastructure sandbox' to help firms innovate and experiment, as well as the introduction of an FCA-led 'CryptoSprint'. The UK government also says that it will be working with the Royal Mint on the creation of an NFT ('as an emblem of the forward-looking approach the UK is determined to take'), and a new Cryptoasset Engagement Group will be convened to work more closely with industry.
- The government has said that it is going to explore ways of enhancing the competitiveness of the UK tax system to encourage more development and overseas input in the cryptoasset market.

Rishi Sunak said:

> 'It's my ambition to make the UK a global hub for cryptoasset technology, and the measures we've outlined today will help to ensure firms can invest, innovate and scale up in this country. [...] We want to see the businesses of tomorrow – and the jobs they create – here in the UK, and by regulating effectively we can give them the confidence they need to think and invest long-term. [...] This is part

10 https://www.gov.uk/government/news/government-sets-out-plan-to-make-uk-a-global-cryptoasset-technology-hub.

> of our plan to ensure the UK financial services industry is always at the forefront of technology and innovation.'

The announcements form part of the overall domestic regulatory developments on the horizon:

- The introduction of a new regulatory regime for stablecoins that are used as a means of payment.
- The introduction of new financial promotion rules in relation to certain high-risk investments including cryptoassets.
- The extension of the financial promotions regime to encompass the promotion of certain types of unregulated cryptoassets.

The first phase of the legislative changes relating to stablecoins focuses on those that are a means of payment. The UK government has described this as its priority. Its January 2021 consultation paper stressed the need to establish a secure regulatory environment for stablecoins, which HM Treasury has identified as having the highest risk exposure (coupled with the fact that stablecoins are most likely to be used as a means of payment as opposed to investment). HM Treasury has said that it will pursue the first phase of regulatory development 'at the earliest opportunity'. The legislative changes contemplated by phase 1 are as follows.

- Amendment of the EMRs and PSRs (to provide the FCA with powers over stablecoin issuers and other entities).
- Extending the application of Part 5 of the Banking Act 2009 (Payment Systems) to include systemic stablecoin-based payment systems.
- Extension of the Financial Services (Banking Reform) Act 2013 to cover stablecoin-based payment systems.
- Expanding the application of the Banking Act 2009 and the Financial Services (Banking Reform) Act 2013 to clarify the entities to which the regulation could apply.
- The introduction of a new regulated custodial activity.

According to HM Treasury:

> 'Taken together, these changes will create the conditions for issuers and service providers of stablecoins used as a means of payment to operate and grow in the UK, in line with the government's firm commitment to place the UK's financial services sector at the forefront of cryptoasset technology and innovation. For consumers, bringing stablecoins into the regulatory framework means they will be able to use stablecoin services with confidence. The government will introduce this legislation when Parliamentary time allows, to deliver a world-leading regulatory regime for stablecoins.'[11]

---

11 HM Treasury Report April 2022 ('UK regulatory approach to cryptoassets, stablecoins, and distributed ledger technology in financial markets: Response to the consultation and call for in evidence'), p 3.

*Chapter 6*

# Overview of financial remedies and the Family Court



## A. INTRODUCTION

**6.01** This chapter provides an overview of the principles that are applied by the courts of England and Wales in matrimonial finance proceedings. It will consider the powers of the court and relevant legislation, principally the Matrimonial Causes Act 1973 ('MCA 1973'), as well as the process of identifying and ascertaining the value of the parties' resources, and the application of the key distributive principles.

## B. THE COURT'S POWERS AND STATUTORY DISCRETION

**6.02** In matrimonial finance proceedings, the court's power is chiefly derived from the MCA 1973. This legislation allows the court to make a variety of financial orders upon the grant of decree of divorce or at any time thereafter up to the point of re-marriage. These can be orders for the settlement and/or transfer of property; periodical payments; lump sums; pension sharing orders; pension attachment orders; secured provision; and the variation of ante-nuptial or post-nuptial settlements.[1] Pension sharing orders, however, are not available on judicial separation.

1 MCA 1973, ss 23–26.

The court has a wide discretion when making such orders on divorce, which for the purposes of this chapter should be construed as including dissolution or annulment of a civil partnership, nullity, and judicial separation.[2]

Section 25 MCA 1973 sets out the factors which the court will have regard to.

Section 25(1) provides that the court will consider 'all the circumstances of the case', with the 'first consideration being given to the welfare while a minor of any child of the family who has not attained the age of eighteen'. The court is required to have regard, in particular, to the factors listed in section 25(2)(a)–(h):

> '(a) the income, earning capacity, property and other financial resources which each of the parties to the marriage has or is likely to have in the foreseeable future, including in the case of earning capacity any increase in that capacity which it would in the opinion of the court be reasonable to expect a party to the marriage to take steps to acquire;
> (b) the financial needs, obligations and responsibilities which each of the parties to the marriage has or is likely to have in the foreseeable future;
> (c) the standard of living enjoyed by the family before the breakdown of the marriage;
> (d) the age of each party to the marriage and the duration of the marriage;
> (e) any physical or mental disability of either of the parties to the marriage;
> (f) the contributions which each of the parties has made or is likely in the foreseeable future to make to the welfare of the family, including any contribution by looking after the home or caring for the family;
> (g) the conduct of each of the parties, if that conduct is such that it would in the opinion of the court be inequitable to disregard it; and
> (h) in the case of proceedings for divorce or nullity of marriage, the value to each of the parties to the marriage of any benefit which, by reason of the dissolution or annulment of the marriage, that party will lose the chance of acquiring.'

As regards the exercise of powers in relation to a child of the family, the court shall, in particular, have regard to the following matters pursuant to section 25(3) MCA 1973:

> '(a) the financial needs of the child;
> (b) the income, earning capacity (if any), property and other financial resources of the child;
> (c) any physical or mental disability of the child;
> (d) the manner in which he was being and in which the parties to the marriage expected him to be educated or trained;
> (e) the considerations mentioned in relation to the parties to the marriage in [Section 25(2)(a),(b),(c) and (e).'

When the court makes a financial order under section 25(2) in favour of a party to the marriage, 'it shall be the duty of the court to consider whether it would be appropriate so to exercise those

2 Civil Partnership Act 2004, Sch 5.

powers that the financial obligations of each party towards the other will be terminated as soon after the grant of the decree as the court considers just and reasonable' (section 25A). This is the so-called 'clean break' principle. When the court considers a party's application for spousal maintenance it has a specific duty to consider whether or not it should order an immediate clean break, ie dismissal of the maintenance application with a direction that the party shall not be able to make any further application for maintenance in relation to the marriage. Where an immediate clean break is not appropriate, the court must consider whether a 'term order' is appropriate, ie an order for a spouse that enables them 'to adjust without undue hardship to the termination of his or her financial dependence on the other party' (section 25A(2) MCA 1973). Such a 'term order' will subsist until a specific timeframe or occasion.

The statute does not explicitly state the objective of the courts or, for obvious reasons, direct the weight to be given to the so-called 'section 25 factors'. However, it has been stated that implicitly the objective must be to achieve a fair outcome:

> 'Section 25A requires the court to consider the appropriateness of a "clean break". Sections 25B-25D, inserted by section 166(1) of the Pensions Act 1995, make provision regarding benefits under pension schemes. They are not material in the present case.
>
> As originally enacted in 1970, in section 5(1) of the Matrimonial Proceedings and Property Act 1970, the list of factors to be taken into account contained a tailpiece. The tailpiece declared what should be the objective of the court when exercising the statutory powers to make financial provision orders and property adjustment orders. The court was so to exercise these powers:
>
> > "as to place the parties, so far as it is practicable and, having regard to their conduct, just to do so, in the financial position in which they would have been if the marriage had not broken down and each had properly discharged his or her financial obligations and responsibilities towards the other."
>
> This tailpiece was later deleted from the legislation, and nothing inserted in its place. In consequence, the legislation does not state explicitly what is to be the aim of the courts when exercising these wide powers. Implicitly, the objective must be to achieve a fair outcome. The purpose of these powers is to enable the court to make fair financial arrangements on or after divorce in the absence of agreement between the former spouses: see Thorpe LJ in Dart v Dart [1996] 2 FLR 286, 294. The powers must always be exercised with this objective in view, giving first consideration to the welfare of the children.'[3]

## C. THE DISTRIBUTIVE PRINCIPLES

**6.03** In the case of *Miller v Miller, McFarlane v McFarlane* three distributive factors were identified in connection with section 25(2) MCA 1973.[4] These are *need*, *compensation*, and *sharing*, which are discussed in turn below.

---

3 *White v White* [2001] 1 AC 596, per Lord Nicholls of Birkenhead.

4 *Miller v Miller, McFarlane v McFarlane* [2006] UKHL 24.

## i. Need

**6.04** The parties' financial needs are assessed having regard to a range of factors including:

- the ages of the parties;
- the parties' earning capacity;
- any physical or mental disability;
- the standard of living enjoyed by the parties during the marriage;
- the length of the marriage;
- the parties' financial obligations;
- the need to maintain a home for the children of the family (and the need to support them).

Most of the needs that will need to be met will have been generated by the marriage:

> '11. This element of fairness reflects the fact that to greater or lesser extent every relationship of marriage gives rise to a relationship of interdependence. The parties share the roles of money-earner, home-maker and child-carer. Mutual dependence begets mutual obligations of support. When the marriage ends fairness requires that the assets of the parties should be divided primarily so as to make provision for the parties' housing and financial needs, taking into account a wide range of matters such as the parties' ages, their future earning capacity, the family's standard of living, and any disability of either party. Most of these needs will have been generated by the marriage, but not all of them. Needs arising from age or disability are instances of the latter.
>
> 12. In most cases the search for fairness largely begins and ends at this stage. In most cases the available assets are insufficient to provide adequately for the needs of two homes. The court seeks to stretch modest finite resources so far as possible to meet the parties' needs. Especially where children are involved it may be necessary to augment the available assets by having recourse to the future earnings of the money-earner, by way of an order for periodical payments.'[5]

The principle of 'needs' has been described as an elastic concept and a 'factor of magnetic importance', as in *McCartney v Mills-McCarney*:

> 'In my judgment, in this case the needs of the wife (generously interpreted) are not simply one of the factors in the case but are a factor of magnetic importance. In a case where the vast bulk of the husband's enormous fortune was made not only before their marriage but also indeed before the wife and husband even met; where the "marital acquest" (if such there has been) is of a very small amount compared to the total assets; where the compensation principle is not in any way engaged; where the marriage is short and where the standard of living lasted only so long as the marriage; where the wife is now and will be very comfortably housed; and where Beatrice's needs are fully assured, surely fairness requires that the wife's needs (generously interpreted) are the dominant factor in the

[5] Ibid, at [11–12].

S.25 exercise. Any other radically different way of looking at this case would, in my judgment, be manifestly unfair.'[6]

In the majority of cases, the assets possessed by the parties will be sufficient to meet the needs of two new households. In April 2018, the Family Justice Council published a second edition of the *Guidance on Financial Needs on Divorce*, which aims to assist the judiciary in relation to cases where needs exceed resources. In other cases where the assets are substantial, 'needs' can be construed as providing sufficient capital and income to maintain an affluent lifestyle.[7]

Save in situations where there is hardship, 'needs' will be causally linked to the marriage:

'18. So far as the "needs" principle is concerned there is an almost unbounded discretion. The main rule is that, save in a situation of real hardship, the "needs" must be causally related to the marriage. Like equity in the old days, the result seems to depend on the length of the judge's foot. It is worth recalling that Heather Mills-McCartney was awarded over £25m to meet her "needs" (McCartney v McCartney [2008] EWHC 401 (Fam)). Mrs Juffali was awarded £62m to meet her "needs" (Juffali v Juffali [2016] EWHC 1684 (Fam)). In the very recent case of AAZ v BBZ [2016] EWHC 3234 (Fam) the court assessed the applicant-wife's "needs" in the remarkable sum of £224m. Plainly "needs" does not mean needs. It is a term of art. Obviously, no-one actually needs £25m, or £62m, or £224m for accommodation and sustenance. The main drivers in the discretionary exercise are the scale of the payer's wealth, the length of the marriage, the applicant's age and health, and the standard of living, although the latter factor cannot be allowed to dominate the exercise.'[8]

## ii. Compensation

**6.05** The principle of compensation arises out of *Miller v Miller*; *McFarlane v McFarlane*.[9] Per Lord Nicholls:

'12. Another strand, recognised more explicitly now than formerly, is compensation. This is aimed at redressing any significant prospective economic disparity between the parties arising from the way they conducted their marriage. For instance, the parties may have arranged their affairs in a way which has greatly advantaged the husband in terms of his earning capacity but left the wife severely handicapped so far as her own earning capacity is concerned. Then the wife suffers a double loss: a diminution in her earning capacity and the loss of a share in her husband's enhanced income. This is often the case. Although less marked than in the past, women may still suffer a disproportionate financial loss on the breakdown of a marriage because of their traditional role as home-maker and child-carer.

6 *McCartney v Mills-McCartney* [2008] EWHC 401 (Fam), at [311].

7 As in *McCartney v Mills-McCartney* [2008] EWHC 401 (Fam); *AAZ v BBZ (No 1)* [2016] EWHC 3234 (Fam).

8 *FF v KF* [2017] EWHC 1093 (Fam) at [18].

9 *Miller v Miller; McFarlane v McFarlane* [2006] UKHL 24.

13. When this is so, fairness requires that this feature should be taken into account by the court when exercising its statutory powers. The Court of Appeal decision in SRJ v DWJ (Financial Provision) [1999] 2 FLR 176, 182, is an example where this was recognised expressly.'

And per Baroness Hale:

'140. A second rationale, which is closely related to need, is compensation for relationship-generated disadvantage. Indeed, some consider that provision for need is compensation for relationship-generated disadvantage. But the economic disadvantage generated by the relationship may go beyond need, however generously interpreted. The best example is a wife, like Mrs McFarlane, who has given up what would very probably have been a lucrative and successful career. If the other party, who has been the beneficiary of the choices made during the marriage, is a high earner with a substantial surplus over what is required to meet both parties' needs, then a premium above needs can reflect that relationship-generated disadvantage.'

The principle serves to compensate any significant financial disparity between the spouses arising out of the way that their marriage was conducted. The compensation principle does not apply where the motivation for a change of career was unrelated to the demands of the marriage. However, sacrificing a career willingly for the family's benefit will not preclude a party from pursuing compensation:

'She is also entitled to a share in the very large surplus, on the principles both of sharing the fruits of the matrimonial partnership and of compensation for the comparable position which she might have been in had she not compromised her own career for the sake of them all. The fact that she might have wanted to do this is neither here nor there. Most breadwinners want to go on breadwinning. The fact that they enjoy their work does not disentitle them to a proper share in the fruits of their labours.'[10]

In the case of *SA v PA (Pre-Marital Agreement: Compensation)*, Mostyn J rejected a compensation argument on the basis that the wife had no track record of the time that she gave up practice as a solicitor to raise a family. The court sought to impose restrictions on the principle:

'Obviously I am bound by the decision of the House of Lords. However, in the light of the later authorities, I think that the principles concerning a compensation claim can properly be expressed as follows:-

i) It will only be in a very rare and exceptional case where the principle will be capable of being successfully invoked.
ii) Such a case will be one where the court can say without any speculation, i.e. with almost near certainty, that the claimant gave up a very high earning career which had it not been foregone would have led to earnings at least equivalent to that presently enjoyed by the respondent.
iii) Such a high earning career will have been practised by the claimant over an appreciable period during the marriage. Proof of this track-record is key.

[10] Ibid, at [154].

iv) Once these findings have been made compensation will be reflected by fixing the periodical payments award (or the multiplicand if this aspect is being capitalised by Duxbury) towards the top end of the discretionary bracket applicable for a needs assessment on the facts of the case. Compensation ought not be reflected by a premium or additional element on top of the needs based award.'[11]

The first principle has been endorsed by the Court of Appeal in *Waggott v Waggott*.[12] In relation to the fourth principle, the Court of Appeal has demonstrated that whilst the court must determine whether (and if so, how) compensation should be addressed to ensure fairness, it is possible to reflect it in a number of different ways.[13]

Compensation arguments face the considerable challenge of evidencing lost career prospects. Other than in high value cases, this distributary principle is frequently eclipsed by the application of needs and sharing principles.

### iii. Sharing

**6.06** The sharing principle provides that both parties to a marriage are equal and therefore the court will normally determine that each spouse is entitled to an equal share of the assets unless there is good reason to the contrary.[14] This was first expressed by Lord Nicholls in *White*, where he identified the imperative of avoiding discrimination against the homemaker in favour of the money-earner. The principle was developed in *Miller v Miller; McFarlane v McFarlane*:

> '16. A third strand is sharing. This 'equal sharing' principle derives from the basic concept of equality permeating a marriage as understood today. Marriage, it is often said, is a partnership of equals. In 1992 Lord Keith of Kinkel approved Lord Emslie's observation that 'husband and wife are now for all practical purposes equal partners in marriage': R v R [1992] 1 AC 599, 617. This is now recognised widely, if not universally. The parties commit themselves to sharing their lives. They live and work together. When their partnership ends each is entitled to an equal share of the assets of the partnership, unless there is a good reason to the contrary. Fairness requires no less. But I emphasise the qualifying phrase: 'unless there is good reason to the contrary'. The yardstick of equality is to be applied as an aid, not a rule.
>
> 17. This principle is applicable as much to short marriages as to long marriages: see Foster v Foster [2003] EWCA Civ 565; [2003] 2 FLR 299, 305, para 19 per Hale LJ. A short marriage is no less a partnership of equals than a long marriage. The difference is that a short marriage has been less enduring. In the nature of things this will affect the quantum of the financial fruits of the partnership.'[15]

---

11 *SA v PA (Pre-Marital Agreement: Compensation)* [2014] EWHC 392 (Fam) at [26].
12 *Waggott v Waggott* [2018] EWCA Civ 727.
13 *H v H* [2014] EWCA Civ 1523.
14 *Charman v Charman (No 4)* [2007] EWCA Civ 503; *Sharp v Sharp* [2017] EWCA Civ 408; and *XW v XH* [2019] EWCA Civ 2262.
15 [2006] UKHL 24.

Baroness Hale in that case provided guidance including a caveat concerning the pooling of assets:

> '153. [...] in a matrimonial property regime which still starts with the premise of separate property, there is still some scope for one party to acquire and retain separate property which is not automatically to be shared equally between them. The nature and the source of the property and the way the couple have run their lives may be taken into account in deciding how it should be shared. There may be other examples. Take, for example, a genuine dual career family where each party has worked throughout the marriage and certain assets have been pooled for the benefit of the family but others have not. There may be no relationship-generated needs or other disadvantages for which compensation is warranted. We can assume that the family assets, in the sense discussed earlier, should be divided equally. But it might well be fair to leave undisturbed whatever additional surplus each has accumulated during his or her working life. However, one should be careful not to take this approach too far. What seems fair and sensible at the outset of a relationship may seem much less fair and sensible when it ends. And there could well be a sense of injustice if a dual career spouse who had worked outside as well as inside the home throughout the marriage ended up less well off than one who had only or mainly worked inside the home.'[16]

As suggested above, the most common justification for an unequal distribution of matrimonial assets is that a greater share to one party is required to meet needs: *Charman v Charman (No 4)*[17]. There are also various factors that may limit the application of the sharing principle. These include:

- conduct;
- the 'special contributions' of the parties;
- any ante-nuptial or post-nuptial agreement;
- identification of property as either matrimonial or non-matrimonial.

Particularly after a long marriage, an asset can have both matrimonial and non-matrimonial features. Whilst non-matrimonial property may be divided in unequal shares the division applied will be contingent on the extent of inter-mingling and the duration of the marriage.[18] In terms of the quantification of the shares, a formulaic approach is not required, and the court's determination will be subject to a cross-check of fairness.[19]

While the sharing principle applies to short marriages and long marriages, the duration of the marriage will affect the quantum of the matrimonial property accrued. However, a variety of factors may come to justify a departure from equality to achieve a fair result. These include a short marriage with no children, separate finances, and dual incomes.[20]

16 Ibid.

17 *Charman v Charman (No 4)* [2007] EWCA Civ 503.

18 *HC v FW* [2017] EWHC 3162 (Fam); *JL v SL (No 2)* [2015] EWHC 360 (Fam); *WX v HX* [2021] EWHC 241 (Fam).

19 *Hart v Hart* [2017] EWCA Civ 1306; *XW v XH* [2017] EWFC 76.

20 *Sharp v Sharp* [2017] EWCA Civ 408.

### iv. The relationship between needs and sharing

**6.07** In terms of how courts navigate the relationship between needs and sharing, in a usual case the first step of the process is to identify and divide the asset base into matrimonial and non-matrimonial property. The matrimonial property is then typically divided equally between the parties. This is subject to an assessment of whether this division results in an overall disposal that is fair and meets needs. If the result is that a party's needs are not met, the remaining non-matrimonial property can be invaded upon to enable those needs to be met.

## D. MATRIMONIAL AND NON-MATRIMONIAL PROPERTY

**6.08** As identified in *Charman v Charman (No 4)*, the court's enquiry in matrimonial finance cases starts with computation of the assets and works through to distribution.[21] The court needs to confirm as at the date of trial what assets are held by the parties and the current value of those assets. The court considers all of the property and financial resources of the parties but draws a distinction between 'matrimonial' and 'non-matrimonial' property. This is not always a clear-cut distinction. Matrimonial property includes property acquired during the marriage through the efforts of one or both parties and includes other assets that were intended to be for joint use or enjoyment irrespective of source. In terms of the application of the sharing principle, it was said in *Charman* that:

> '66. To what property does the sharing principle apply? The answer might well have been that it applies only to matrimonial property, namely the property of the parties generated during the marriage otherwise than by external donation; and the consequence would have been that non-matrimonial property would have fallen for redistribution by reference only to one of the two other principles of need and compensation to which we refer in paragraph 68 below. Such an answer might better have reflected the origins of the principle in the parties' contributions to the welfare of the family; and it would have been more consonant with the references of Baroness Hale in Miller at [141] and [143] to "sharing … the fruits of the matrimonial partnership" and to "the approach of roughly equal sharing of partnership assets". We consider, however, the answer to be that, *subject to the exceptions identified in Miller to which we turn in paragraphs 83 to 86 below, the principle applies to all the parties' property but, to the extent that their property is non-matrimonial, there is likely to be better reason for departure from equality*. It is clear that both in White at p.605 F-G and in Miller at [24] and [26] Lord Nicholls approached the matter in that way; and there was no express suggestion in Miller, even on the part of Baroness Hale, that in White the House had set too widely the general application of what was then a yardstick.' [emphasis added].

---

21 [2007] EWCA Civ 503.

As suggested above, where 'needs' do not arise, the starting point is usually that matrimonial assets will be shared and divided equally, while non-matrimonial assets will remain in the contributor's possession.

In the case of *Hart v Hart*, the Court of Appeal addressed the method by which the non-matrimonial property should be considered.[22] The authority outlines a three-stage process that should be followed in cases engaging this issue:

> '88. The principle which is being applied is that the sharing principle applies with force to matrimonial property and with limited or no force to non-matrimonial property. How should this principle be applied in practice when the existence of non-matrimonial property is being asserted?
>
> 89. First, a case management decision will need to be made as whether, and if so what, proportionate factual investigation is required. As the Supreme Court said in Wyatt v Vince [2015] 1 FLR 972 (paragraph 29) the overriding objective requires the court to manage financial remedy proceedings cases actively and to identify those issues which need full investigation and those which do not. This was reiterated in Sharland v Sharland [2015] 2 FLR 1367 in which Lady Hale refers to there being "enormous flexibility to enable the procedure to fit the case" (paragraph 43).
>
> 90. It may be, for example, that the external contribution can immediately be seen to be sufficiently insignificant in the context of the case that it warrants no further enquiry. It may be, at the other end of the spectrum, that there is clearly no matrimonial property so that there is also no need to undertake any further factual investigation. In other words, if the facts clearly demonstrate the existence of a "sharp dividing line" the court will use that line for the purposes of determining what award to make. If, on the other hand, the enquiry would require an account to be undertaken of the marriage and/or some other expensive investigation and/or would be of "doubtful utility", the court could be expected to decide that such an enquiry was neither proportionate nor required to enable the court to achieve a fair outcome. If some further enquiry is warranted, the court will have to determine what "degree of particularity or generality" is required. Where, in the spectrum, any particular case lies is for the court to decide.
>
> 91.Secondly, the court will need to make such factual decisions as the evidence enables it to make. In this context, I do not agree with Mostyn's comment in N v F that a party would need to prove the existence of pre-marital assets "by clear documentary evidence" (paragraph 24). There is no reason to limit the form or scope of the evidence by which the existence of such property can be established. The normal evidential rules apply. These include the court's ability to draw inferences if such are warranted.
>
> 92. The court may decide that the non-marital contribution is not sufficiently material or bears insufficient weight to justify a finding that any property is non-matrimonial.
>
> 93. Alternatively, if the evidence establishes a clear dividing line between matrimonial and non-matrimonial property, the court will obviously apply that differentiation at the next, discretionary stage.

22 [2017] EWCA Civ 1306.

94. If, however, at the other end of the spectrum, there is a complicated continuum, it would be neither proportionate nor feasible to seek to determine a clear line. C v C was an example of such a case. In those circumstances the court will undertake a broad evidential assessment and leave the specific determination of how the parties' wealth should be divided to the next stage. As I have said, where in the spectrum a case lies depends on the circumstances of the case and is for the judge to decide.

95. The third and final stage of the process is when the court undertakes the section 25 discretionary exercise. Even if the court has made a factual determination as to the extent of the parties' wealth which is matrimonial property and that which is not, the court still has to fit this determination into the exercise of the discretion having regard to all the relevant factors in this case. This is not to suggest that, by application of the sharing principle, the court will share non-matrimonial property but the court has an obligation to determine that its proposed award is a fair outcome having regard to all the relevant section 25 factors.

96. If the court has not been able to make a specific factual demarcation but has come to the conclusion that the parties' wealth includes an element of non-matrimonial property, the court will also have to fit this determination into the section 25 discretionary exercise. The court will have to decide, adopting Wilson LJ's formulation of the broad approach in Jones, what award of such lesser percentage than 50% makes fair allowance for the parties' wealth in part comprising or reflecting the product of non-marital endeavour. In arriving at this determination, the court does not have to apply any particular mathematical or other specific methodology. The court has a discretion as to how to arrive at a fair division and can simply apply a broad assessment of the division which would affect "overall fairness". This accords with what Lord Nicholls said in Miller and, in my view, with the decision in Jones.

97. Finally, I would repeat that fairness has a broad horizon. I recognise, of course, the need for clear guidance and principles when the court is given a discretion as wide as that contained in section 25 of the 1973 Act. Such clarity not only assists judges when determining financial claims but also enables those seeking to resolve the consequences of their separation and divorce, as it has been described, "to bargain in the shadow of the law": Matrimonial Property, Needs and Agreements 2014 (Law Com No 343) paragraph 3.6. However, this should not lead to the imposition of constraints which are not needed to achieve, and which deprive the court of the flexibility required to achieve, a fair outcome.'

In terms of examples of matrimonial property, in most cases the matrimonial home and its contents will constitute matrimonial property. This is particularly likely to be the case where the spouses have both contributed and/or it is held in joint names.

Assets that have been acquired during the marriage as a result of combined efforts are also likely to constitute matrimonial property. Those efforts need not be of a financial character. Mostyn J in *JL v SL (No 2)* described matrimonial property as: 'the property which the parties have built up by their joint (but inevitably different) efforts during the span of their partnership. It should be divided equally. This principle is reflected in statutory systems in other jurisdictions. It resonates with moral and philosophical values. It promotes equality and banishes discrimination.'[23]

23 [2015] EWHC 360 (Fam) at [18].

## E. SPECIAL CONTRIBUTIONS

**6.09** The doctrine of the 'special contribution' arose from *Cowan v Cowan* where Thorpe LJ observed that 'fairness certainly permits and in some cases requires recognition of the product of the genius with which one only of the spouses may be endowed'.[24] This is sometimes deployed as an argument to justify an unequal division of matrimonial assets in favour of originators of substantial wealth. Having been considered again in *Lambert v Lambert*,[25] the doctrine later formed part of the House of Lords' decision in *Miller v Miller; McFarlane v McFarlane*,[26] per Lord Nicholls:

> '67. On this I echo the powerful observations of Coleridge J in G v G (Financial Provision: Equal Division) [2002] EWHC 1339 (Fam); [2002] 2 FLR 1143, 1154–1155, paras 33–34. Parties should not seek to promote a case of 'special contribution' unless the contribution is so marked that to disregard it would be inequitable. A good reason for departing from equality is not to be found in the minutiae of married life.'

Lady Hale also drew a comparison between contributions and the Court's approach to conduct:

> '145. Is there any need to qualify these aims, considered in the light of all the circumstances and the factors listed in section 25(2)? Two which have emerged in later cases should, in my view, be firmly rejected: conduct and special contributions. Section 25(2)(g) is quite clear: the court has to have regard to the parties' conduct if it would be inequitable to disregard it. In the olden days, when all the assets were assumed to be the breadwinner's and he was making an allowance to enable his wife to live separately from him, the wife's conduct might reduce the allowance she would otherwise have needed or even extinguish it altogether. She had therefore to be 100% blameless in order to be sure of her conventional one-third share of his income. In theory, if she were 50% to blame, her share might be halved, although in practice the divorce courts were more flexible than that (but see, for example, the approach in Ackerman v Ackerman [1972] Fam 1, where a wife who was assessed as 25% to blame for the breakdown of the marriage was subject to a 25% discount from what she would otherwise have received). But once the assets are seen as a pool, and the couple as equal partners, then it is only equitable to take their conduct into account if one has been very much more to blame than the other: in the famous words of Ormrod J in Wachtel v Wachtel [1973] Fam 72, at p 80, the conduct had been 'both obvious and gross'. This approach is not only just, it is also the only practicable one. It is simply not possible for any outsider to pick over the events of a marriage and decide who was the more to blame for what went wrong, save in the most obvious and gross cases. Yet in Miller v Miller, both Singer J and the Court of Appeal took into account the parties' conduct, even though it fell far short of this. In my view they were wrong to do so.
>
> 146. In my view, the question of contributions should be approached in the much the same way as conduct. Following White v White [2001] 1 AC 596, the search was on for some reason to stop short

24 *Cowan v Cowan* [2001] EWCA Civ 679, at [67].
25 *Lambert v Lambert* [2002] EWCA Civ 1685.
26 [2006] UKHL 24.

of equal sharing, especially in 'big money' cases where the capital had largely been generated by the breadwinner's efforts and enterprise. There were references to exceptional or 'stellar' contributions: see Cowan v Cowan [2001] EWCA Civ 679; [2002] Fam 97. These, in the words of Coleridge J in G v G (Financial Provision: Equal Division) [2002] EWHC 1339 (Fam); [2002] 2 FLR 1143, at p 1154, opened a 'forensic Pandora's box'. As he pointed out, at p 1155:

> "[W]hat is 'contribution' but a species of conduct? ... Both concepts are compendious descriptions of the way in which one party conducted him/herself towards the other and/or the family during the marriage. And both carry with them precisely the same undesirable consequences. First, they call for a detailed retrospective at the end of a broken marriage just at a time when parties should be looking forward, not back .... But then, the facts having been established, they each call for a value judgment of the worth of each side's behaviour and translation of that worth into actual money. But by what measure and using what criteria? ... Is there such a concept as an exceptional/special domestic contribution or can only the wealth creator earn the bonus? ... It is much the same as comparing apples with pears and the debate is about as sterile or useful."

146. A domestic goddess self-evidently makes a 'stellar' contribution, but that was not what these debates were about. Coleridge J's words were rightly influential in the later retreat from the concept of special contribution in Lambert v Lambert [2002] EWCA Civ 1685; [2003] Fam 103. It had already been made clear in White v White [2001] 1 AC 596 that domestic and financial contributions should be treated equally. Section 25(2)(f) of the 1973 Act does not refer to the contributions which each has made to the parties' accumulated wealth, but to the contributions they have made (and will continue to make) to the welfare of the family. Each should be seen as doing their best in their own sphere. Only if there is such a disparity in their respective contributions to the welfare of the family that it would be inequitable to disregard it should this be taken into account in determining their shares.'

The treatment of 'special contributions' was also considered more recently by the Court of Appeal in *Work v Gray*.[27] The Court endorsed the summary of the law set out by Holman J at first instance[28] (subject to one amendment), as follows:

'1. The characteristics or circumstances which would result in a departure from equality have to be of a wholly exceptional nature such that it would very obviously be inconsistent with the objective of achieving fairness for them to be ignored: per Bodey J in Lambert but quoted with obvious approbation by Lord Nicholls of Birkenhead in Miller at paragraph 68.
2. Exceptional earnings are to be regarded as a factor pointing away from equality of division when, but only when, it would be inequitable to proceed otherwise (Lord Nicholls of Birkenhead in Miller at paragraph 68).
3. Only if there is such a disparity in their respective contributions to the welfare of the family that it would be inequitable to disregard it should this be taken into account in determining their shares (Baroness Hale of Richmond, in Miller at paragraph 146).
4. It is extremely important to avoid discrimination against the home-maker (the Court of Appeal in Charman at paragraphs 79 and 80).

27 *Work v Gray* [2017] EWCA Civ 270.
28 [2015] EWHC 834 (Fam) at [140].

5. The amount of the wealth alone may be so extraordinary as to make it easy for the party who generated it to claim an exceptional and individual quality which deserves special treatment. Often, however, he or she will need independently to establish such a quality, whether by genius in business or some other field (the Court of Appeal in Charman at paragraph 80). A windfall is not enough.
6. There is no identified threshold for such a claim to succeed (the Court of Appeal in Charman at paragraph 88).'

## F. INCOME

**6.10** As was submitted in *Waggott v Waggott*,

> 'the 1973 Act contains a "statutory steer" towards a clean break when this can be fairly achieved. There is an "assumption" that the marital partnership does not stay alive for the purposes of sharing future resources unless justified by either need and/or by application of the compensation principle. The objective is "independent finances and self-sufficiency" and an "equal start on the road to independent living" not continuing economic parity or equivalence.'[29]

However, periodical payments can be awarded by the court in circumstances where they are required to meet needs or for compensation.

The relevant principles at play were summarised by Mostyn J in *SS v NS (Spousal Maintenance)* as follows:[30]

'1. A spousal maintenance award is properly made where the evidence shows that choices made during the marriage have generated hard future needs on the part of the claimant. Here the duration of the marriage and the presence of children are pivotal factors.
2. An award should only be made by reference to needs, save in a most exceptional case where it can be said that the sharing or compensation principle applies.
3. Where the needs in question are not causally connected to the marriage the award should generally be aimed at alleviating significant hardship.
4. In every case the court must consider a termination of spousal maintenance with a transition to independence as soon as it is just and reasonable. A term should be considered unless the payee would be unable to adjust without undue hardship to the ending of payments. A degree of (not undue) hardship in making the transition to independence is acceptable.
5. If the choice between an extendable term and a joint lives order is finely balanced the statutory steer should militate in favour of the former.
6. The marital standard of living is relevant to the quantum of spousal maintenance but is not decisive. That standard should be carefully weighed against the desired objective of eventual independence.

---

29 [2018] EWCA Civ 727 at [58].

30 *SS v NS (Spousal Maintenance)* [2014] EWHC 4183 (Fam) at [46].

7. The essential task of the judge is not merely to examine the individual items in the claimant's income budget but also to stand back and to look at the global total and to ask if it represents a fair proportion of the respondent's available income that should go to the support of the claimant.
8. Where the respondent's income comprises a base salary and a discretionary bonus the claimant's award may be equivalently partitioned, with needs of strict necessity being met from the base salary and additional, discretionary, items being met from the bonus on a capped percentage basis.
9. There is no criterion of exceptionality on an application to extend a term order. On such an application an examination should to be made of whether the implicit premise of the original order of the ability of the payee to achieve independence had been impossible to achieve and, if so, why.
10. On an application to discharge a joint lives order an examination should be made of the original assumption that it was just too difficult to predict eventual independence.
11. If the choice between an extendable and a non-extendable term is finely balanced the decision should normally be in favour of the economically weaker party.'

## G. SUMMARY

**6.11** Many of the threads described in this chapter were recently drawn together in the decision of Peel J in *WC v HC*[31] which merits reading in full. The authority provides a helpful overview of many aspects of the law applied in matrimonial finance proceedings:

'21. The general law which I apply is as follows:

i) As a matter of practice, the court will usually embark on a two-stage exercise, (i) computation and (ii) distribution; Charman v Charman [2007] EWCA Civ 503.

ii) The objective of the court is to achieve an outcome which ought to be "as fair as possible in all the circumstances"; per Lord Nicholls at 983H in White v White [2000] 2 FLR 981.

iii) There is no place for discrimination between husband and wife and their respective roles; White v White at 989C.

iv) In an evaluation of fairness, the court is required to have regard to the s25 criteria, first consideration being given to any child of the family.

v) S25A is a powerful encouragement towards a clean break, as explained by Baroness Hale at [133] of Miller v Miller; McFarlane v McFarlane [2006] 1 FLR 1186.

vi) The three essential principles at play are needs, compensation and sharing; Miller; McFarlane.

vii) In practice, compensation is a very rare creature indeed. Since Miller; McFarlane it has only been applied in one first instance reported case at a final hearing of financial remedies, a decision of Moor J in RC v JC [2020] EWHC 466 (although there are one or two examples of its use on variation applications).

viii) Where the result suggested by the needs principle is an award greater than the result suggested by the sharing principle, the former shall in principle prevail; Charman v Charman.

31 *WC v HC* [2022] EWFC 22, 2022 WL 00845769.

ix) In the vast majority of cases the enquiry will begin and end with the parties' needs. It is only in those cases where there is a surplus of assets over needs that the sharing principle is engaged.

x) Pursuant to the sharing principle, (i) the parties ordinarily are entitled to an equal division of the marital assets and (ii) non-marital assets are ordinarily to be retained by the party to whom they belong absent good reason to the contrary; Scatliffe v Scatliffe [2017] 2 FLR 933 at [25]. In practice, needs will generally be the only justification for a spouse pursuing a claim against non- marital assets. As was famously pointed out by Wilson LJ in K v L [2011] 2 FLR 980 at [22] there was at that time no reported case in which the applicant had secured an award against non-matrimonial assets in excess of her needs. As far as I am aware, that holds true to this day.

xi) The evaluation by the court of the demarcation between marital and non-martial assets is not always easy. It must be carried out with the degree of particularity or generality appropriate in each case; Hart v Hart [2018] 1 FLR 1283. Usually, non-marital wealth has one or more of 3 origins, namely (i) property brought into the marriage by one or other party, (ii) property generated by one or other party after separation (for example by significant earnings) and/or (iii) inheritances or gifts received by one or other party. Difficult questions can arise as to whether and to what extent property which starts out as non-marital acquires a marital character requiring it to be divided under the sharing principle. It will all depend on the circumstances, and the court will look at when the property was acquired, how it has been used, whether it has been mingled with the family finances and what the parties intended.

xii) Needs are an elastic concept. They cannot be looked at in isolation. In Charman (supra) at [70] the court said:

> "The principle of need requires consideration of the financial needs, obligations and responsibilities of the parties (s.25(2)(b); of the standard of living enjoyed by the family before the breakdown of the marriage (s.25(2)(c); of the age of each party (half of s.25(2)(d); and of any physical or mental disability of either of them (s.25(2)(e)".

xiii) The Family Justice Council in its Guidance on Financial Needs has stated that:

> "In an appropriate case, typically a long marriage, and subject to sufficient financial resources being available, courts have taken the view that the lifestyle (i.e "standard of living") the couple had together should be reflected, as far as possible, in the sort of level of income and housing each should have as a single person afterwards. So too it is generally accepted that it is not appropriate for the divorce to entail a sudden and dramatic disparity in the parties' lifestyle."

xiv) In Miller/McFarlane Baroness Hale referred to setting needs "at a level as close as possible to the standard of living which they enjoyed during the marriage". A number of other cases have endorsed the utility of setting the standard of living as a benchmark which is relevant to the assessment of needs: for example, G v G [2012] 2 FLR 48 and BD v FD [2017] 1 FLR 1420.

xv) That said, standard of living is not an immutable guide. Each case is fact- specific. As Mostyn J said in FF v KF [2017] EWHC 1093 at [18];

> "The main drivers in the discretionary exercise are the scale of the payer's wealth, the length of the marriage, the applica.nt's age and health, and the standard of living, although the latter factor cannot be allowed to dominate the exercise".

xvi) I would add that the source of the wealth is also relevant to needs. If it is substantially non-marital, then in my judgment it would be unfair not to weigh that factor in the balance. Mostyn J made a similar observation in N v F [2011] 2 FLR 533 at [17–19].

**The Law: Pre-Marital and Post-Marital Agreements**

22. I do not need to look beyond Radmacher v Granatino [2010] UKSC 42 from which the following essential propositions can be drawn:

i) There is no material distinction between an ante-nuptial agreement and a post- nuptial agreement (para 57).

ii) If an ante-nuptial agreement, or indeed a post-nuptial agreement, is to carry full weight, "what is important is that each party should have all the information that is material to his or her decision, and that each party should intend that the agreement should govern the financial consequences of the marriage coming to an end" (para 69).

iii) It is to be assumed that each party to a properly negotiated agreement is a grown up and able to look after himself or herself (para 51).

iv) The first question will be whether any of the standard vitiating factors, duress, fraud or misrepresentation, is present. Even if the agreement does not have contractual force, those factors will negate any effect the agreement might otherwise have. But unconscionable conduct such as undue pressure (falling short of duress) will also be likely to eliminate the weight to be attached to the agreement, and other unworthy conduct, such as exploitation of a dominant position to secure an unfair advantage, would reduce or eliminate it (para 71). The court may take into account a party's emotional state, and what pressures he or she was under to agree. But that again cannot be considered in isolation from what would have happened had he or she not been under those pressures. (Para 72).

v) The court should give effect to a nuptial agreement that is freely entered into by each party with a full appreciation of its implications unless in the circumstances prevailing it would not be fair to hold the parties to their agreement. (para 75).

**The Law: inter vivos subvention**

23. I addressed this topic in M v M [2020] EWFC 41 where I said as follows:

"65. Should a court inquire into the willingness of the wider family to assist one or both spouses?

66. To my mind there are 2 main categories of cases:

(i) Where a spouse has an interest in an asset together with other family members, and the court frames its order so as to " judiciously encourage" the other family members to assist in extraction by the spouse of value referable to his or her interest. The court should not cross the boundary of improper pressure in so doing. This is the so-called Thomas v Thomas doctrine (Thomas v Thomas [1995] 2 FLR 668). Importantly, it applies when the spouse has an actual interest in an asset shared with third parties (e.g. family) but is confronted by liquidity difficulties.

(ii) Where family members, who are gratuitous donors, are willing to make funds available by gift or loan to the relevant spouse. In this instance, the spouse has no legal or beneficial interest; it is a pure act of generosity for a person under no obligation to do so.

68. [In respect of the second category] I apply the following principles:

(i) The starting point is that there is absolutely no obligation on a third-party family member to provide funds from his or her personal resources. As Holman J vividly said in Luckwell v Limata [2014] EWHC 502 at para 6: " I wish to stress with the utmost clarity that neither the wife's father nor her mother are under the slightest legal obligation whatsoever to pay a single penny to, or for, their daughter, nor their grandchildren, nor, still less, their son-in-law." This statement is wholly consistent with law and fairness. The court's function is to distribute the parties' resources, not the resources of wider families; see paras 66 and 67 of Alireza v Radwan [2017] EWCA Civ 1545.

(ii) That said, on occasions wider family members may show themselves prepared to assist, willingly and under no pressure from the court to do so. Two distinct scenarios spring to mind;

    (a) Whether a spouse's family will be likely, if requested, to come to his or her aid in meeting specific needs personal to the spouse in question and;

    (b) Whether a spouse's family will be likely, if requested, to come to his or her aid in making a payment to the other spouse to assist in bringing financial remedy proceedings to a conclusion.

(iii) The first scenario is not uncommon. If means are available, the wider family, although under no legal obligation to do so, may willingly help with buying a house or meeting income needs if the alternative is homelessness and penury. But the evidence of willingness to do so must be clear. Mere speculation, or optimistic assumption, is insufficient.

(iv) The second scenario is rarer, for obvious reasons, although it can unlock cases and bring about settlement. For example, the family of a spouse may offer to pay the receiving spouse a lump sum to avoid sale of the marital home. Again, in my judgment, there must be clear evidence to justify such a finding. Speculation and optimistic assumption will not suffice.

(v) The court should not place pressure on the third party who is perfectly entitled to decline to provide support. As Deputy High Court Judge Nicholas Mostyn QC (as he was then) said in TL v ML [2005] EWHC 2860 at para 101:

> "The correct view must be this. If the court is satisfied on the balance of probabilities that an outsider will provide money to meet an award that a party cannot meet from his absolute property then the court can, if it is fair to do so, make an award on that footing. But if it is clear that the outsider, being a person who has only historically supplied bounty, will not, reasonably or unreasonably, come to the aid of the payer then there is precious little the court can do about it."

    The judge was there addressing the second of my suggested two scenarios, but in my view his remarks apply with equal force to the first scenario.

(vi) In either scenario, where the evidence shows, to the requisite standard of proof, that third party family members will likely provide financial support to one or other of the spouses, that, in my judgment, constitutes a resource that a court is entitled to take into account. To do otherwise would be artificial. As to the sort of evidence which the court will evaluate when deciding upon the likelihood of future assistance:

    (a) Usually, the court will look to see whether bounty has been provided in the past, in what quantity and over what amounts of time, as evidence of a pattern.

(b) Additionally, the court can look at specific offers of long-term future financial support made to a spouse before or after marital breakdown.

(c) Offers of interim provision to tide the spouse over with assistance towards legal fees and income needs during the period of litigation will be of very limited evidential relevance to the question of whether long- term future support will be forthcoming. Usually, such payments are transitory in nature, designed to assist the recipient spouse with the demands of the litigation.

(d) Absent clear evidence establishing (i) a track record of historic payment and/or (ii) reliable representations of future subvention, the court will be hard pressed to be satisfied of this class of resource."

**The Law: inheritance**

24. In Alireza v Radwan [2018] 1 FLR 1333 King LJ reviewed the principles pertaining to inherited wealth, including where forced heirship applies.

"32. The first question therefore is 'does the wife's father's wealth/ the wife's inheritance prospects constitute a financial resource which she has or is likely to have in the foreseeable future?'"

33. Mr Peel says not and reminds the court that in the ordinary course of events a party's inheritance prospects are disregarded by the court. In Michael v Michael [1986] 2 FLR 389 Nourse LJ said (at 395):

> "I am of the clear opinion that s.25(2)(a) of the Act of 1973 as amended, whilst it is primarily concerned with property and financial resources in which there is a vested or contingent interest, is not exclusively so concerned. Indeed, its broad and somewhat informal language demonstrates that it was intended to operate at large and not in some strait-jacket tailored to the sober uniforms of property law. Thus, there can be no doubt that it could in certain circumstances extend to something which in the language of the law is a mere expectancy or spes successionis, for example and interest which might be taken under the will of a living person."

34. Nourse LJ went on to give an example of a case where there was clear evidence that a person had a terminal illness, that property was left to the respondent in his will and that it was highly improbable the testator would revoke the will. Having given such an example he went on (at 396)

> ".... However those facts, being extremely special demonstrate that the occasions on which such an interest will fall within s.25(2)(a) of the Act of 1973 as amended, are likely to be rare. In the normal case uncertainties both as to the fact of inheritance and as to the times at which it will occur will make it impossible to hold that the property is property which is likely to be had in the foreseeable future."

35. Mr Todd for his part relies on the decision of Munby J (as he then was) in C v C (ancillary relief trust fund) (C v C) [2010] 1 FLR 337.

36. In C v C the husband had a vested interest in property in that, upon the death of his widowed step mother, he and his three siblings would inherit an estate as tenants in common in equal shares. This was not a discretionary trust. The trustees had no power to appoint 'even a farthing' [19] to the husband except with the written consent of the widow who could give it or withhold at her 'unfettered and uncontrolled' discretion. As Munby J said:

> "... and the husband and the court have to take the widow as they find her. As against the widow there can be no question of exerting any 'judicious encouragement' (see Thomas v Thomas [1995]

> 2 FLR 668 at 670), as there might be if what was in issue was the exercise by the trustees of their powers if they had any that were relevant."

37. Given that the husband's interest was vested and the likelihood was that the reversion would fall in in about 15 years (that being the actuarial life expectancy of the widow), Munby J concluded:

> "I confess that on this crucial issue my mind has wavered. On any view, as it seems to me, this case is at or very close to the outer extremity of what can properly be considered a 'financial resource' which a spouse is 'likely to have in the foreseeable future'. At best it is, to adopt Cumming-Bruce LJ's metaphor, only dimly visible. But on balance I have concluded that … the husband's interest is indeed such a resource. In other words, I am persuaded though I have to say without much enthusiasm, that the question posed … is to be answered in the affirmative."

38. Munby J said that his decision would have been different had the likelihood been of the husband receiving substantially less than the current value of the estate on the death of the widow, or had the widow's life expectancy been greater than he found it to be. Munby J went on to put his decision that the husband's vested interest was a resource in context:

> "[66] I must emphasise that, consistently with the terms of the preliminary issue, all I have decided is that the husband's interest in the trust fund is a 'financial resource' which he is 'likely to have in the foreseeable future'. I have not decided that it would in fact be appropriate to make an order of the kind made in Priest v Priest and Milne v Milne or, indeed, appropriate to make any order at all in relation to his interest in the trust fund. All I have decided is that his interest in the trust fund is, within the meaning of s 25(2)(a), a 'financial resource' which he is 'likely to have in the foreseeable future', and, accordingly, something which s 25(2) requires the judge at the final hearing to 'have regard to'. Having had regard to it, the judge may decide to make some order in relation to the husband's interest under the trust. On the other hand, the judge, having had regard to it, may decide not to make any order at all in relation to the husband's interest under the trust. It is entirely a matter for the judge who is called upon, as I have not been, to exercise the discretion conferred by ss 24 and 25."

39. In my judgment the words of Nourse LJ in Michael hold good 30 years on and in the ordinary course of events uncertainties both as to the fact of inheritance and as to the times at which it will occur, will make it impossible to hold that an inheritance prospect is property which is "likely to be had in the foreseeable future."

40. The present case is different. The wife's inheritance prospects do not have the inherent uncertainty found where a will is made in a country such as England where there is no concept of forced heirship. In my view, a prospective inheritance which has the certainty brought to it by the laws of forced heirship, is capable of being a "financial resource" which the wife "has or is likely to have in the foreseeable future".

41. Mr Peel sought to persuade the court that there remained uncertainties which should mean that, notwithstanding the forced heirship laws, the court should disregard the wife's inheritance prospects. He suggested by way of example that the father could give all his money away to charity or there could be some sort of cataclysmic political event which would mean he would lose his wealth. There was

no evidence before the court to that effect and the wife chose not to call her father to give evidence. In those circumstances a court would be entitled to conclude, as the judge did, that a portion of the father's estate would indeed come to the wife in 16+years.

42. Having said that, as Munby J explained in C v C, all that such a finding does is to conclude that the prospective inheritance is a section 25(2)(a) resource; it does not mean that it is inevitably appropriate for the court to make an order whereby the meeting of the needs of the wife is in any way dependant on the prospective inheritance.'

*Chapter 7*

# Cryptocurrency as a matrimonial asset



## A. INTRODUCTION

**7.01** In civil litigation, the legal status of cryptocurrency and whether it constitutes 'property' is of importance because it impacts the recourse a party may have in circumstances of wrongdoing (typically in situations of fraud or ransomware attacks). In family law, the question of whether cryptocurrencies are regarded as 'property' in law has importance because 'property' is statutory language contained in *inter alia* sections 24 and 25 of the Matrimonial Causes Act ('MCA 1973'). If cryptocurrencies (and cryptoassets generally) *are* 'property', they will constitute one of the factors that the court will have regard to pursuant to section 25(2)(a) and 25(3)(b). Likewise, it is necessary to know whether they can be the subject of, for example, a property adjustment order under section 24, or alternatively an order for periodical payments, a legal services payment order, or other forms of interim relief, such as a freezing order. This is an area of jurisprudence and legislative thinking that has evolved markedly in the past few years, and which has been the subject of numerous civil authorities discussed below. It must be noted that these are decisions concerning interim relief rather than the substantive proceedings, and the rulings as to the status of cryptoassets as 'property' should be viewed in that interlocutory context.

## B. ARE CRYPTOCURRENCIES 'PROPERTY' AND WHY DOES IT MATTER?

**7.02** As has been referred to in earlier parts of this work, the UK Jurisdiction Taskforce's ('UKJT') 'Legal Statement on the Status of Cryptoassets and Smart Contracts' (November 2019) heralded a more confident treatment of cryptoassets as 'property' in the courts of England and Wales.

The UKJT's statement, which merits reading in full, opens with discussion of the term 'property', to which the authors attribute a strict definition of not constituting a thing itself but rather a legal relationship with a thing. Citing *Yanner v Eaton*, property is described as a way of describing a power recognised in law as permissibly exercised over the thing.[1] In other words, the fundamental proprietary relationship is that of *ownership*: the owner of a thing is broadly entitled to exercise control over it and enjoy it to the exclusion of anybody else. That said, ownership is merely one kind of property right: property is a comprehensive term that can be used to describe many kinds of relationship between a person and a subject matter.[2]

*English law divides property (as distinct from real property) into two conventional classifications: chose in possession and chose in action.* The former is a 'thing' that one can have physical possession of, while the latter is a property right that can be obtained or enforced through legal action.

At first blush, cryptocurrency is neither: it is not a physical thing (it is essentially data). Nor does a cryptocurrency such as Bitcoin create a right against anybody; unlike, for example, money in a bank account which gives rise to a relationship of debtor and creditor. A cryptocurrency is an intangible asset that does not depend on a legal right enforceable against a third party in order to have intrinsic value. On this view, cryptocurrency is information or data, which various English authorities suggest does not constitute 'property'.

Why does it matter if a cryptoasset is capable of being property? According to the UKJT:

> 'It matters because in principle proprietary rights are recognised against the whole world, whereas other personal rights are recognised only against someone who has assumed a relevant legal duty. Proprietary rights are of particular importance in an insolvency, where they generally have priority over claims by creditors, and when someone seeks to recover something that has been lost, stolen or unlawfully taken. They are also relevant to the questions of whether there can be a security interest in a cryptoasset and whether a cryptoasset can be held on trust.
>
> The term property is also part of the lexicon of the law: it is widely used in statutes and cases. It is important to understand whether the many statutory and common law rules applicable to property apply also to cryptoassets, and, if so, how. Of particular significance are the rules concerning succession on death, the vesting of property in personal bankruptcy, the rights of liquidators in corporate insolvency, and tracing in cases of fraud, theft or breach of trust. It would, to say the least, be highly unsatisfactory if rules of that kind had no application to cryptoassets.
>
> In some cases, what matters is not, or not only, whether a thing is property but whether it is a specific type of property. For example, certain proprietary remedies, such as conversion or lien, are available only in respect of things in possession (tangible property that can be the subject of physical possession

---

1 *Yanner v Eaton* [1999] HCA 53 at [17-20].
2 Ibid.

and so physical control). More generally, whether a thing is property, or a type of property, depends on the context and the reason why the question is being asked. A thing may be property for one legal purpose but not for another; and some statutes expressly broaden or narrow the scope of what they treat as property.'

The UKJT concluded that whether English law treats a particular cryptoasset as property ultimately depends on the nature of the asset, the rules of the system in which it exists, and the purpose for which the question is asked. That being said, the Taskforce concluded that:

'i. Cryptoassets have all the indicia of property.
ii. The novel or distinctive features possessed by some cryptoassets – intangibility, cryptographic authentication, use of a distributed transaction ledger, decentralisation, rule by consensus – do not disqualify them from being property.
iii. Cryptoassets are not disqualified from being property as pure information, or because they might not be classifiable either as things in possession or things in action.
iv. Cryptoassets are therefore to be treated in principle as property.
v. However, a private key is not in itself to be treated as property because it is information.'[3]

Prior to the publication of this watershed statement, the courts of England and Wales had already taken steps in the direction of recognising cryptoassets as property that can be susceptible to interim relief, particularly freezing orders.

*Vorotyntseva v Money-4 Ltd (T/A Nebeus.com) and others* concerned an application brought ex parte on short notice for a freezing order.[4] The claimant sought a freezing order against Money-4 Ltd (trading as Nebeus.com) and two of its directors, one of whom was sole shareholder of the business. The claimant's case was that she gave the business a substantial quantity of Bitcoin and Ethereum (293.6583085 Bitcoin and 400.39984802 Ether, which together were worth, as at 24 August 2018, approximately £1.5 million). The funds were to be dealt with on the claimant's behalf and the purpose of the transaction was to test Nebeus's trading platform. The claimant became concerned that the funds had been dissipated and so her solicitors asked specifically for confirmation that they had not been, and moreover that were still in the possession of Nebeus and would be held by them. The confirmation was not forthcoming and as a consequence the claimant brought an application for a freezing order.

The claimant was offered an undertaking to maintain the cryptocurrency pending further order.

The defendants provided information in the form of emails with screenshots from a computer screen. This evidence was challenged by the claimant, who asserted that in respect of the screenshot concerning the Bitcoin, that did not in fact confirm on its own that her Bitcoins were

---

3 At [85-86]. A pdf of the report is available at: https://technation.io/lawtech-uk-resources/#cryptoassets.
4 *Vorotyntseva v Money-4 Ltd (T/A Nebeus.com) and others* [2018] EWHC 2596 (Ch).

still being held by Nebeus. The other document confirmed the Ethereum. That evidence was challenged on the basis that it appeared to have been altered:

> 'The other document is the Ethereum document. I have been provided with a paper copy and also with an iPad to show what appears on a computer screen. The resolution on the iPad is better than the paper copy. It can be seen that the relevant Ether address starts with the letters OX7B1B and continues on in the way that these sorts of cryptographic hash strings do. However then what appears to have happened is that the claimant's name, Elena Vorotyntseva, and a date, appears to have been superimposed on top in typescript (with a blurred border). It does appear to me, as Mr. Ramsden submits, that this document which has been produced by the first respondent is a composite of something that is on the relevant computer screen and then something else that has been overlayed on top of it, in order to make the composite look as though Mrs Vorotyntseva's name appears on the screenshot, when in fact it does not.'[5]

Mr Justice Birss emphasised that these inferences could only ever be preliminary based on the material that had been produced.

It was submitted on behalf of the claimant that the concerns over the evidence substantiated her concern about the risk of dissipation. The judge accepted that submission and agreed that there was a real risk of dissipation in the case. Despite all possible allowances having been made for the defendants given the very short notice of the application, the judge nevertheless concluded that very serious questions arose from the material that the defendants had provided. On that basis the freezing order was granted. The court did not interrogate the question of whether cryptocurrencies constitute 'property', which was not a contested point:

> 'Another point taken on the freezing order relates to the terms of the proprietary order. The point is that the Bitcoin and the Ethereum currency is ultimately said to belong to the claimant and not to the respondents. I should say no suggestion has been made by the respondents that the cryptocurrency that was given to them does not belong to the claimant. Nor is there any suggestion that cryptocurrency cannot be a form of property or that a party amenable to the court's jurisdiction cannot be enjoined from dealing in or disposing of it. I am satisfied that the court can make such an order, if it is otherwise appropriate.'[6]

In *Robertson v Persons Unknown*,[7] the Commercial Court granted an asset preservation order over Bitcoin finding that there was a serious issue to be tried concerning a proprietary claim. The claimant was the victim of a 'spear phishing' attack. The email account of a firm in which Mr Robertson was making a personal investment had been hacked and Mr Robertson's intended investment of 100 Bitcoin (then worth a sum in the region of £1.2 million) was misdirected to the wrongdoers. Having used the services of Chainalysis it was established that 80 Bitcoins had been sent to a wallet held at Coinbase UK Ltd, the UK entity of San Francisco-based

---

5 Ibid, at [7].
6 Ibid, at [13].
7 Unreported, CL-2019-000444.

Coinbase (a crypto exchange). The claimant applied for: (i) a freezing order against persons unknown in respect of 100 Bitcoin; (ii) an asset preservation order over the 80 Bitcoin that had been traced to the Coinbase wallet; and (iii) a Bankers Trust order to reveal the identity of that wallet holder.

At the first *ex parte* hearing, Moulder J was not prepared to proceed on the basis that the unknown wallet holder was the wrongdoer or even part of the fraud. Accordingly, she was not prepared to make the freezing order against that unidentified wallet holder who could have been an innocent third party. Despite the strong evidence of fraud, the judge was not satisfied that the balance of convenience or risk of dissipation requirements of the legal test had been met to justify the making of a freezing order against 'persons unknown'. However, Moulder J did consider the submission that the claimant had a proprietary claim over the 80 Bitcoin and proceeded on the basis that Bitcoin could be personal property.[8] For the purpose of a proprietary injunction (asset preservation order), Moulder J identified a key issue was being whether legal title remained with the claimant. She noted:

> 'So if this turns out to be an effective transfer of title because it is a personal – an item of personal property with a right of possession, it could have been transferred.'

The judge referred to the conclusion of the Financial Markets Law Committee (FMLC), in its report 'Issues of Legal Uncertainty Arising in the Context of Virtual Currencies' (July 2016), that cryptocurrencies may be conveniently understood as being a type of hybrid virtual chose in possession. If that were right, then, as the Court observed, the claimant would not have a better title than any recipient of the 80 Bitcoin if the recipient were a *bona fide* purchaser for value. Likewise, sale of goods legislation provides other defences that might enable a recipient of cryptocurrencies to defeat a proprietary claim, but only if cryptocurrencies are treated as choses in possession.

The claimant submitted that Bitcoin are not choses in possession and that, based on *Armstrong DLW GmbH v Winnington Networks Ltd*,[9] for the purpose of advancing a proprietary restitutionary claim and obtaining an interlocutory asset preservation order, it did not matter whether the Court treated them as choses in action or some form of other intangible property. Ultimately the Court proceeded on that basis and granted the asset preservation order which prevented any dealings with the 80 Bitcoin or any instructions being given to the crypto exchange to transfer them. The Court also ordered the Bankers Trust orders which enabled Coinbase to disclose information about the wallet holder.[10]

---

8 NB The judgement in the *Vorotyntseva* case had not been published at the time that the *Robertson* case was heard.

9 *Armstrong DLW GmbH v Winnington Networks Ltd* [2012] EWHC 10 (Ch).

10 'Time to clarify the legal status of cryptocurrencies?', Stewarts Law LLP, 12 November 2019, https://www.stewartslaw.com/news/legal-status-of-cryptocurrencies/ and 'A Bitcoin first? Stewarts obtains asset preservation order over cryptocurrency',

The current key authority following the UKJT's 'Legal Statement on Cryptoassets and Smart Contracts' is the case of *AA v Persons Unknown & Ors*.[11] The interim proprietary injunction ordered in that case followed the application of an English insurer (AA) of a Canadian company which had fallen victim to the BitPaymer ransomware virus. AA had paid a ransom on behalf of its insured customers to secure access and use of that customer's systems which had been disabled using the malware. The effect of the malware was that the insured customer's computer systems became encrypted, the virus having bypassed the system's firewalls and antivirus software. The insured customer received 'notes' left on the encrypted system by the wrongdoers (the first defendant, Persons Unknown) demanding payment. Given the importance of access to the customer's systems, AA paid a ransom of approximately US$950,000 in Bitcoin in exchange for a decryption tool. On transfer of the Bitcoin, the decryption tool was provided, and access was restored. Once the files had been recovered, the claimant sought to recover the ransom. Investigators were able to trace 96 Bitcoin to an address (owned or controlled by the second defendant, identity unknown) linked to the cryptocurrency exchange known as Bitfinex and operated by two BVI companies (the third and fourth defendants). The remainder of the Bitcoin had been transferred into fiat currency. The purpose of the application was to assist the insurer in its recovery of the Bitcoin. It sought a proprietary injunction based on claims of restitution and/or constructive trust.

The key question for the court was whether for the purposes of granting interim relief in the form of an interim proprietary injunction that cryptocurrencies are a form of property capable of being the subject of a proprietary injunction. Drawing on the UKJT's statement, Bryan J concluded that they were:

> '55. Turning then to the relevant principles in relation to the granting of a proprietary injunction, the first and perhaps fundamental question that arises in relation to this claim for a proprietary injunction is whether or not in fact the Bitcoins, which are being held in this account of the second defendant with the third or fourth defendants are property at all. Prima facie there is a difficulty in treating Bitcoins and other crypto currencies as a form of property: they are neither chose in possession nor are they chose in action. They are not choses in possession because they are virtual, they are not tangible, they cannot be possessed. They are not choses in action because they do not embody any right capable of being enforced by action. That produces a difficulty because English law traditionally views property as being of only two kinds, choses in possession and choses in action. In *Colonial Bank v Whinney* [1885] 30 Ch.D 261 Fry LJ said:
>
> > "All personal things are either in possession or action. The law knows no *tertium quid* between the two."

Stewarts Law LLP, 20 August 2019, https://www.stewartslaw.com/news/cryptocurrency-bitcoin-asset-preservation-order-stewarts/. The Cybersecurity team at Stewarts Law LLP, led by Marc Jones, represented the claimant in *Robertson v Persons Unknown* (Unreported, CL-2019-000444).

11 *AA v Persons Unknown & Ors* [2019] EWHC 3665 (Comm).

56. On that analysis Bitcoins and other crypto currencies could not be classified as a form of property, which would prevent them being the subject of a proprietary injunction or a freezing injunction. This exact issue has recently in November 2019 been the subject of detailed consideration by the UK Jurisdictional Task Force ("UKJT") which has published a legal statement on Crypto assets and Smart contracts, ("the Legal Statement"). The UKJT is chaired by Sir Geoffrey Vos, and Sir Antony Zacaroli is also a member. However, neither in their judicial capacity was responsible for the drafting of the legal statement, nor have either in their judicial capacities endorsed that legal statement. Indeed Sir Geoffrey Voss explained in the foreword to the Legal Statement: "It is not my role as a judge nor that of the UKJT or its parent, the UK Lawtech Delivery Panel, to endorse the contents of the Legal Statement". Those responsible for drafting the Legal Statement were Laurence Akka QC, David Quest QC, Matthew Lavy and Sam Goodman.

57. It follows that the legal statement is not in fact a statement of the law. Nevertheless, in my judgment, it is relevant to consider the analysis in that Legal Statement as to the proprietary status of crypto currencies because it is a detailed and careful consideration and, as I shall come on to, I consider that that analysis as to the proprietary status of crypto currencies is compelling and for the reasons identified therein should be adopted by this court.

58. The difficulty identified in treating crypto currencies in property, as I say, starts from the premise that the English law of property recognises no forms of property other than choses in possession and choses in action. As I have already identified, crypto currencies do not sit neatly within either category. However, on a more detailed analysis I consider that it is fallacious to proceed on the basis that the English law of property recognises no forms of property other than choses in possession and choses in action. The reasons for this are set out between paragraphs 71 to 84 in the Legal Statement.

*"71. The Colonial Bank case concerned a dispute about shares deposited as security for a loan. The borrower was declared bankrupt and there was a contest for the shares between the plaintiff bank and the trustee in bankruptcy. The case was not about the scope of property generally: there was no dispute that the shares were property. The relevant question was rather whether they were things in action within the meaning of the Bankruptcy Act 1883, an issue of statutory interpretation. If so, then they were excluded from the bankrupt estate by section 44 of that Act.*

*72. Lindley LJ and Cotton LJ held that the shares were not things in action. They relied principally on previous case law where the court had come to a similar conclusion in relation to the predecessor statute, the Bankruptcy Act 1869. They also drew some support from sections 50(3) and 50(5) of the 1883 Act, which appeared to make a distinction between shares and things in action.*

*73. Fry LJ reached the opposite conclusion, reasoning principally from what he considered to be the essential nature of a share. A share constituted "the right to receive certain benefits from a corporation, and to do certain acts as a member of that corporation" and was therefore, in his view, closely akin to a debt. He supported his conclusion by a comparison of shares to other, established, things in action, such as partnership interests and interests in funds.*

*74. Fry LJ's statement that "personal things" are either in possession or in action, and that there is no third category, may carry the logical implication that an intangible thing is not property if it is not a thing in action. It is not clear, however, whether Fry LJ intended that corollary and it should not in any case be regarded as part of the reasoning leading to his decision (and so binding in other cases). The question before him was whether the shares were things in action for the purpose of the Bankruptcy Act, not whether they were property, still less the scope of property generally.*

*75. Moreover, in making the statement Fry LJ attributed a very broad meaning to things in action. He approved a passage from Personal Property by Joshua Williams, which described things in action as a kind of residual category of property: "In modern times [sc. by the 19th century] ... several species of property have sprung up which were unknown to the common law ... For want of a better classification, these subjects of personal property are now usually spoken of as ... [things] in action. They are, in fact, personal property of an incorporeal nature ... ".*

*76. On appeal, the House of Lords also framed the question as one about statutory interpretation. They reversed the Court of Appeal's decision, approving the judgment and reasoning of Fry LJ. They did not explicitly address the issue of exhaustive classification between things in action and things in possession and said nothing about the definition of property. Lord Blackburn did say, however, that "in modern times lawyers have accurately or inaccurately used the phrase '[things] in action' as including all personal chattels that are not in possession". Thus, to the extent that the House of Lords agreed with Fry LJ on the classification issue, that seems to have been on the basis that the class of things in action could be extended to all intangible property (i.e. it was a residual class of all things not in possession) rather than on the basis that the class of intangible property should be restricted to rights that could be claimed or enforced by action.*

*77. Our view is that Colonial Bank is not therefore to be treated as limiting the scope of what kinds of things can be property in law. If anything, it shows the ability of the common law to stretch traditional definitions and concepts to adapt to new business practices (in that case the development of shares in companies).*

*78. Colonial Bank was referred to in Allgemeine Versicherungs-Gesellschaft Helvetia v Administrator of German Property by Slesser LJ as showing "how the two conditions of [thing] in action and [thing] in possession are antithetical and how there is nomiddle term". Again, however, the case was not about the scope of property generally but about whether something that was undoubtedly property should be classified as a thing in possession or a thing in action.*

*79. Most recently, Colonial Bank was cited in 2014 in Your Response v Datateam. In that case, the claimant sought to assert a lien over a database in digital form but faced the obstacle of the previous decision of the House of Lords in OBG Ltd v Allan that there could be no claim in conversion for wrongful interference with a thing in action because it could not be possessed. In an attempt to distinguish the case from OBG, the claimant argued that, even if the database could not be regarded as a physical object, it was a form of intangible property different from a thing in action and so was capable of being possessed.*

*80. The Court of Appeal rejected the argument. Moore-Bick LJ said that Colonial Bank made it "very difficult to accept that the common law recognises the existence of intangible property other than [things] in action (apart from patents, which are subject to statutory classification), but even if it does, the decision in OBG Ltd v Allan [2008] 1 AC 1 prevents us from holding that property of that kind is susceptible of possession so that wrongful interference can constitute the tort of conversion." He said that there was "a powerful case for reconsidering the dichotomy between [things] in possession and [things] in action and recognising a third category of intangible property, which may also be susceptible of possession and therefore amenable to the tort of conversion" but the Court of Appeal could not do that because it was bound to follow the decision in OBG. The other members of the court agreed.*

*81. The Court of Appeal did not, and did not need to, go so far as to hold that intangible things other than things in action could never be property at all, only that they could not be the subject of certain remedies. The intangible thing with which they were concerned was a database, which (as Floyd LJ said) would not be regarded as property anyway because it was pure information. They did not have to consider intangible assets with the special characteristics possessed by cryptoassets.*

*82. In other cases, the courts have found no difficulty in treating novel kinds of intangible assets as property. Although some of those cases are concerned with the meaning of property in particular statutory contexts, there are at least two concerning property in general. In Dairy Swift v Dairywise Farms Ltd, the court held that a milk quota could be the subject of a trust; and in Armstrong v Winnington, the court held that an EU carbon emissions allowance could be the subject of a tracing claim as a form of "other intangible property", even though it was neither a thing in possession nor a thing in action.*

*83. A number of important 20th century statutes define property in terms that assume that intangible property is not limited to things in action. The Theft Act 1968, the Proceeds of Crime Act 2002, and the Fraud Act 2006 all define property as including things in action "and other intangible property". It might be said that those statutes are extending the definition of property for their own, special purposes, but they at least demonstrate that there is no conceptual difficulty in treating intangible things as property even if they may not be things in action. Moreover, the Patents Act 1977 goes further in providing, at s30, that a patent or application for a patent "is personal property (without being a thing in action)". That necessarily recognises that personal property can include things other than things in possession (which a patent clearly is not) and things in action.*

*84. We conclude that the fact that a cryptoasset might not be a thing in action on the narrower definition of that term does not in itself mean that it cannot be treated as property."*

59. The conclusion that was expressed was that a crypto asset might not be a thing in action on a narrow definition of that term, but that does not mean that it cannot be treated as property. Essentially, and for the reasons identified in that legal statement, I consider that a crypto asset such as Bitcoin are property. They meet the four criteria set out in Lord Wilberforce's classic definition of property in *National Provincial Bank v Ainsworth* [1965] AC 1175 as being definable, identifiable by third parties, capable in their nature of assumption by third parties, and having some degree of permanence. That too, was the conclusion of the Singapore International Commercial Court in *B2C2 Limited v Quoine PTC Limited* [2019] SGHC (I) 03 [142].

60. There are also two English authorities to which my attention has been drawn where crypto currencies have been treated as property, albeit that those authorities do not consider the issue in depth. They are, and I have already mentioned them, in *Vorotyntseva v Money -4 Limited t/a as Nebeus.com*, the decision of Birss J, where he granted a worldwide freezing order in respect of a substantial quantity of Bitcoin and Ethereum, another virtual currency, and the case of *Liam David Robertson*, where Moulder J granted an asset preservation order over crypto currencies in that case.

> 61. In those circumstances and for the reasons I have given, as elaborated upon in the Legal Statement which I gratefully as what I consider to be an accurate statement as to the position under English law, I am satisfied for the purpose of granting an interim injunction in the form of an interim proprietary injunction that crypto currencies are a form of property capable of being the subject of a proprietary injunction.'

This area of the law regarding cryptocurrencies is developing. *AA v Persons Unknown* is regarded as the main authority for the principle that Bitcoin and other cryptocurrencies can be considered property under English law and can therefore be the subject of a proprietary injunction.

In *Toma and another v Murray*, the court considered an application to continue a without notice interim injunction preventing the defendant from dealing with Bitcoin held in a specific account. The claimants had sold Bitcoin through an account based in Finland.[12] The payment that had been received for the Bitcoin was, however, reversed, and the claimants were left without either the funds or the Bitcoin. The defendant accepted that he had control of the accounts which had been used to make and withdraw the payments and that a fraud of some variety had taken place. He asserted that his account had been hacked. The claimants brought an action seeking to recover the value of the Bitcoin held in the defendant's coin depot account and were granted a without notice interim injunction. At the return date they applied to continue the injunction. The claimants accepted that they were unable to satisfy a cross-undertaking in damages but asserted that as their claim was a proprietary tracing claim it reduced the significance of damages as an adequate remedy. The defendant submitted that as he had an unencumbered property in Dublin in his possession, damages would be an adequate remedy. He also highlighted the volatility of Bitcoin and the risk of loss in a situation where he would be prevented from selling the cryptocurrency in appropriate circumstances.

The court refused the application to continue the interim injunction preventing the defendant from dealing with Bitcoin in the coin depot account. The purpose of an interim injunction was to mitigate the risk of injustice to the claimants between the making of their claim and trial, but that had to be weighed against the risk of injustice to the defendant. Applying *AA v Persons Unknown*,[13] the first point of consideration was whether there was a serious issue to be tried, and if so, the court needed to consider where the balance of convenience sat in light of the adequacy of damages as an adequate remedy, the giving of a cross-undertaking in damages, and the merits of the proposed claim. Here the court held that though there was a serious issue to be tried, it was not necessary to conduct a mini-trial or express a view as to the allegations of fraud and/or hacking of the account. An arguable case for a proprietary remedy did not mean that the court would inevitably grant a proprietary injunction. The court also considered *Haiti v Duvalier*

12 *Toma and another v Murray* [2020] EWHC 2295 (Ch).

13 [2019] EWHC 3556 (Comm).

*(Mareva Injunction) (No.2)*[14] and *National Commercial Bank Jamaica Ltd v Olint Corp Ltd* and held that in principle, damages would be an adequate remedy, even if that meant converting a proprietary tracing claim into a personal remedy of the value of the Bitcoin sold.[15] It could not be said that the defendant would be unable to meet an award against him, given that he owned valuable property. On the other hand, the claimants would be unable to pay a cross-undertaking in damages. The effect of this was heightened by the implications of the volatility of Bitcoin. On that basis the injunction was discharged.

In *Ion Science Limited v Persons Unknown and others* (unreported, 21 December 2020), the court considered an ex parte interim application which involved allegations of fraud in relation to a cryptocurrency initial coin offering ('ICO').[16] A company registered in England and Wales, Ion Science Limited, and its sole director and shareholder, Duncan Johns, claimed that they have been the victims of an ICO fraud. They asserted that they had been induced by the persons unknown (who had claimed to be connected to a supposed Swiss entity called Neo Capital) to transfer the sum of £588,002 in the form of some 64.36 Bitcoin in the belief that they were making investments in real cryptocurrency products. The claimants submitted that Neo Capital was not a real company; that it did not appear on the Swiss equivalent of the Companies House register; and that the Swiss financial services regulator had issued a warning that it may be providing unauthorised services, and that it has no presence online beyond a website. The other respondents were Binance Holdings (a Cayman company that the claimants believed to be the parent of the group of companies operating the Binance cryptocurrency exchange), and Payment Ventures, a US entity believed to be the parent of the group of companies operating the Kraken cryptocurrency exchange. The claimants sought to secure the assets, namely the Bitcoin or traceable proceeds thereof, which they considered to have been misappropriated, and to preserve the assets of the Neo Capital individuals pending enforcement. They also wanted to reveal the true identity of the Neo Capital individuals so that an effective remedy could be sought against them. Accordingly, the claimants sought a proprietary injunction, a worldwide freezing order, and an ancillary disclosure order against the persons unknown. They also sought a disclosure order pursuant to the Bankers Trust jurisdiction and/or pursuant to Civil Procedure Rule (CPR) 25.1(g) against the two cryptocurrency exchanges. Thirdly, the claimants sought permission to serve out of jurisdiction and by alternative means. The hearing was held in private because of the risk of tipping off and/or the possibility that a public hearing might frustrate the object of the relief pursued.

Butcher J ordered the relief sought on the ex parte application. In terms of the proprietary injunction, the judge was satisfied that there was a prima facie case of wrongdoing and that the there was no evidence before the court that the individuals in question would be able to satisfy a monetary judgment for what was as considerable sum. Deciding whether the injunction should

---

14 *Haiti v Duvalier (Mareva Injunction) (No.2)* [1990] 1 QB 202.
15 *National Commercial Bank Jamaica Ltd v Olint Corp Ltd* [2009] UKPC 16.
16 *Ion Science Limited v Persons Unknown and others* CL-2020-000840.

be ordered also required consideration of whether it was just and convenient to grant the order. Butcher J held that it was because of material before the court which indicated that the applicants had been the victims of an extensive cyber fraud.

In terms of the worldwide freezing order, the judge found that there was a good arguable case on the merits as well as a real risk of dissipation. The latter was based on the nature of the claim as well as the assumed wrongdoers' conduct which involved, if the claimants' evidence was accurate, the use of aliases and apparently false documents, as well as the nature of Neo Capital which was not a registered entity and was on a regulator's warning list. Although, unlike in an ordinary case, there was no identification of assets that could be caught by the order, Butcher J observed that this was a typical feature of a persons unknown case and should not be a bar to the granting of a freezing order in this variety of case. The court held that the grant of a worldwide freezing order was just and convenient in order to assist the victims of what appeared to be a significant and prolonged cyber fraud.

In terms of the Bankers Trust orders, Butcher J was satisfied as to the basis on which the court could permit service out of the jurisdiction of a claim for such relief, even where no positive remedy was sought from the respondent other than information. The judge also referred to *MacKinnon v Donaldson, Lufkin and Jenrette Securities Corporation*, which envisaged that a Bankers Trust order might be once where there can be service out of the jurisdiction in exceptional circumstances, which could include cases of 'hot pursuit'. This was such a case.[17]

The *Ion Science* case reinforces previous interim rulings that suggest that cryptoassets *can* be treated as 'property':

> 'First of all, I am satisfied that there is at least a serious issue to be tried that cryptoassets such as bitcoin are property within the common law definition of that term. There are a number of decisions, albeit on interim applications, which have come to that view, those being based, at least in part, on the analysis in the UK Jurisdiction Task Force statement on Cryptoassets and Smart Contracts. It is also right to mention that the same conclusion was reached in New Zealand in the case of *Ruscoe v Cryptopia Ltd (in liquidation)* [2020] NZHC 782.'[18]

The authority is also noteworthy in that in the discussion of leave to serve out of jurisdiction and the associated question of whether there was a serious issue to be tried, *the Court found that the lex situs of a cryptoasset is the place where the person or company who owns it is domiciled.*

> '12. The first substantive issue which requires consideration is as to whether there is jurisdiction over the first defendant / respondent; in other words, the persons unknown. Of course, the applicants do not

17 *MacKinnon v Donaldson, Lufkin and Jenrette Securities Corporation* [1986] Ch 482.

18 *Ion Science Limited v Persons Unknown and others*, 21 December 2020 (Commercial Court) CL-2020-000840.

know where the individuals are located. They are, accordingly, seeking permission to serve them out of the jurisdiction on the basis that some or all of those individuals may neither be present nor domiciled in England and Wales. In order to obtain leave to serve out, the court has to be satisfied that there is a serious issue to be tried on the merits, that there is a good arguable case that the claims fall within one of the gateways under CPR PD 6B, and that England is the appropriate forum for the trial of the dispute.

13. As to the first of those, whether there is a serious issue to be tried on the merits, I am satisfied that the applicants can show at least a serious issue to be tried on the merits of their claims, those claims being brought or intimated in deceit, unlawful means conspiracy and by way of an equitable proprietary claim. As to the first of those, deceit, it is important to consider at the outset the question of what would be the governing law of the claim. I am satisfied that there is at least a serious issue to be tried that it is English law pursuant to Article 4.1 of Rome II on the basis that England was the place where the damage occurred, either on the simple basis that the bank account which funded the Coinbase account was an English account or that the asset was taken from the claimants' control in England and Wales, because Mr Johns granted remote access to his computer which was in England and Wales; or alternatively because the relevant bitcoin were located in England and Wales prior to the transfer. The second of those aspects is on the basis that the lex situs of a cryptoasset is the place where the person or company who owns it is domiciled. That is an analysis which is supported by Professor Andrew Dickinson in his book *Cryptocurrencies in Public and Private Law* at para.5.108. There is apparently no decided case in relation to the lex situs for a cryptoasset. Nevertheless, I am satisfied that there is at least a serious issue to be tried that that is the correct analysis.

14. As to the elements of a claim in deceit, I am satisfied that there is a serious issue to be tried that the relevant defendant, the first respondent, as they have been called, made representations which were false, which they knew were untrue or were reckless as to their truth, intending that those representations would induce the claimants and which did in fact induce the claimants to act by way of making or allowing the payments to be made, as a result of which the claimants suffered loss. I am also satisfied that there is a serious issue to be tried that the claimants have a claim in unlawful means conspiracy; and that there is a serious issue to be tried as to an equitable proprietary claim in respect of the bitcoin which were transferred on the basis that the property was obtained by fraud and was held on trust for the victim of the fraud, or on the basis that there was a Quistclose trust in that the moneys were paid for a specific purpose which has failed. The transferors were, at least on the basis of the material which has been put before me, told that the moneys to be paid would be held and applied for a specific purpose only and the relevant sums were transferred on that basis. I also consider that in relation to the question of the availability of a gateway within PD 6B that the applicants can show a good arguable case that the tort claims fall within Gateway 9 as either the damage was sustained within the jurisdiction or was sustained as a result of acts committed within the jurisdiction, namely the making of representations to Mr Johns, the transfer of funds and the granting of remote access to Mr Johns' computer in England.

15. The equitable proprietary claim can be said to fall within Gateway 15 as being a claim made against the defendant as constructive trustee or as trustee of a resulting trust where the claim arises out of acts committed or events occurring within the jurisdiction or relates to assets within the jurisdiction, the relevant acts on this basis occurring within the jurisdiction, namely the making of or the reliance on representations and the transfer of funds or the granting of access to Mr Johns's computer, and the claim

relates to assets which, on the basis of the argument which I have mentioned, have their lex situs within the jurisdiction.

16. Finally in relation to the proper forum, in a case of a persons unknown claim it is obviously difficult to identify another forum, but here in addition to that simple point that the claimants are domiciled in England and Wales, the relevant funds were transferred from England and Wales, the relevant bitcoin are or certainly were located in England and Wales and also the documents are in English and the witnesses are based in England, at least on the claimants' side. For all of those reasons, I am satisfied for the purposes of this application that it has been shown that England is the proper forum for the trial of the claimants' claims.'[19]

In a similar vein, in *Fetch.ai Ltd and another v Persons Unknown Category A and others*, the Circuit Commercial Court granted a proprietary injunction, worldwide freezing order, and ancillary disclosure order against 'persons unknown', along with Bankers Trust orders against the fourth and fifth respondents (related cryptocurrency exchange companies) and a Norwich Pharmacal order against the fifth respondent.[20] Intriguingly, HHJ Pelling QC (sitting as a judge of the High Court) did not recognise a tension between the ambiguous categorisation of cryptocurrencies as either *chose in action* or *chose in possession*. The Court proceeded on the basis of the former:

'I am satisfied that the assets credited to the first applicant's accounts on the Binance Exchange are to be regarded as property for the purposes of English law. They are, to put it no higher for present purposes, a chose in action, and a chose in action, as a matter of English law, is generally regarded as property. That is an important consideration when considering claims against those located out of the jurisdiction as I explain below.'[21]

Accordingly, there is a string of authority and growing judicial confidence in the civil courts that cryptocurrency constitutes 'property' as a matter of law, and all that that implies. While we do not yet have a Family Court authority addressing the point, it is the view of the authors that the aforementioned cases together provide compelling authority should the contrary be asserted in a matrimonial finance context. It must be noted, however, that the aforementioned decisions concern interim relief rather than the substantive proceedings, and the rulings as to the status of cryptoassets as 'property' must be seen in that interlocutory context.

In the recent case of *Lavinia Deborah Osbourne v (1) Persons Unknown (2) Ozone Networks Inc. trading as Opensea*[22] (unreported, April 2022), the High Court of England and Wales ordered an urgent interim injunction in respect of two NFTs. The NFTs represented two unique

19 At [12-16].
20 *MacKinnon v Donaldson, Lufkin and Jenrette Securities Corporation* [2021] EWHC 2254 (Comm).
21 At [9].
22 *Lavinia Deborah Osbourne v (1) Persons Unknown (2) Ozone Networks Inc. trading as Opensea* [2022] EWHC 1021 (Comm).

digital artworks from the Boss Beauties series removed from the claimant's MetaMask wallet without her knowledge or consent in January 2022. The judgment recognises the proprietary rights of NFT holders at a time when these cryptoassets are increasingly being misappropriated. At the return hearing on 31 March 2022, HHJ Pelling QC granted another injunction until further order.[23]

This is believed to be the first reported case of a proprietary injunction being deployed in relation to an NFT as a standalone asset, separate from the underlying 'thing' that it represents. The Court held that for the purposes of the application, NFTs have all the indicia of property and so are capable of forming the subject of the injunction. The judgement states the following at [13]–[17]:

> '13. I am satisfied on the basis of the evidence available that the claimant has demonstrated a good arguable case that she has been defrauded of the non-fungible tokens to which she refers in her evidence. There is clearly going to be an issue at some stage as to whether non-fungible tokens constitute property for the purposes of the law of England and Wales, but I am satisfied on the basis of the submissions made on behalf of the claimant that there is at least a realistically arguable case that such tokens are to be treated as property as a matter of English law.
>
> 14. The other factor which is material to this claim is where such tokens are to be treated as being located as at the time when they were lost. As is apparent from the limited description I have already given, non-fungible tokens are in effect a stream of electrons resulting in a credit item to a crypto account. As such, insofar as they have a physical manifestation at all, that is likely to be where the servers relevant to the account are maintained. However, attempting to litigate issues such as this by reference to a concept as ethereal as that would be difficult or impossible.
>
> 15. Unsurprisingly, therefore, in a series of cases relating to crypto currency fraud, it has been consistently held that crypto assets, are to be treated as located at the place where the owner of them is domiciled. There is no reason at any rate at this stage to treat non fungible tokens in any other way, assuming for present purposes as I do that they are to be treated as property as a matter of English law.
>
> 16. This approach has been adopted in any number of cases, including at least two, if not three, decided by me. All these cases follow what Butcher J said in *Ion Science Ltd v Persons Unknown and others* (unreported) [2020] (Comm), a judgment delivered on 21 December 2020 in the Commercial Court, where at paragraph 15, Butcher J held that the lex situs of a crypto asset is the place where the person or company who owns it is domiciled, adopting the analysis contained in Professor Andrew Dickinson's book on crypto currencies and public and private law. I consider I should follow these cases in relation to the asset the subject of these proceedings. Therefore, and for these purposes, the claimant is to be treated as having had the non-fungible tokens in her possession in England by operation of that principle.'

---

23 https://36group.co.uk/news/2022/4/landmark-nft-judgment.

## C. ARE CRYPTOCURRENCIES DIVISIBLE?

**7.03** One of the attractive features of cryptocurrency is that it is, in principle, divisible. Cryptocurrency can usually be broken down into smaller units. The units themselves will depend on the cryptocurrency in question.

For Bitcoin, as the value of a single coin has increased, so too has the usage of increasingly small fractions of the digital currency. Bitcoin is divided into units as small as 0.00000001 BTC, which makes it attractive for micropayments. At the time of writing, 0.001 BTC is worth £23.54. The smallest value supported by the Bitcoin network is the 'satoshi', named after Satoshi Nakamoto, the creator of Bitcoin. Each bitcoin can be broken down into one-hundred-million (100,000,000) satoshis. In the future, if required, the divisibility of bitcoin can be increased to 100 billion smaller parts or even more, as the Bitcoin protocol and its related software can be modified to handle even smaller units. Another common unit is the bit or microbitcoin (μBTC), which corresponds to one millionth (0.000 001) of a bitcoin. Bits, like most fiat currencies, have a two-decimal precision. Due to the network's limited accuracy, you can send 1.23 bits but not 1.234 bits.

The chart below from SpectroCoin outlines the most commonly referred-to measurements, ranging in value from the smallest amount of bitcoin (Satoshi) to the greatest (Megabit – MBTC).[24]

| Bitcoin denomination | Bitcoin units | Value |
|---|---|---|
| Satoshi | SAT | 0.000 000 01 BTC |
| Microbit | μBTC (uBTC) | 0.000 001 BTC |
| Millibit | mBTC | 0.001 BTC |
| Centibit | cBTC | 0.01 BTC |
| Decibit | dBTC | 0.1 BTC |
| Bitcoin | BTC | 1 BTC |
| DecaBit | daBTC | 10 BTC |
| Hectobit | hBTC | 100 BTC |
| Kilobit | kBTC | 1000 BTC |
| Megabit | MBTC | 1 000 000 BTC |

## D. DISCLOSURE ON FORM E

**7.04** There is an ongoing duty to provide full, frank, and clear disclosure in financial remedy proceedings.[25]

24 https://spectrocoin.com/en/faqs/bitcoins/is-bitcoin-divisible.html.

25 *J v J* [1955] P 215; *Baker v Baker* [1995] 2 FLR 829; *US v SR* [2014] EWHC 175 (Fam).

Failure to disclose ownership of cryptocurrency, or to assist appropriately in any disclosure or valuation process relating to it could be considered to be litigation conduct.

As noted by Roberts J in *AB v CD*, it is not for a litigant to judge the ambit or consequences of disclosure. Any information that is relevant to the outcome must be disclosed.[26] Failure to do so may well result in an order for costs.[27]

As identified by Mostyn J in *NG v SG*, where the court is satisfied that the disclosure given by one party has been materially deficient then:

i) The court is duty bound to consider by the process of drawing adverse inferences whether funds have been hidden.
ii) But such inferences must be properly drawn and reasonable. It would be wrong to draw inferences that a party has assets which, on an assessment of the evidence, the court is satisfied he has not got.
iii) If the court concludes that funds have been hidden then it should attempt a realistic and reasonable quantification of those funds, even in the broadest terms.
iv) In making its judgment as to quantification the court will first look to direct evidence such as documentation and observations made by the other party.
v) The court will then look to the scale of business activities and at lifestyle.
vi) Vague evidence of reputation or the opinions or beliefs of third parties is inadmissible in the exercise.
vii) The *Al-Khatib v Masry*[28] technique of concluding that the non-discloser must have assets of at least twice what the claimant is seeking should not be used as the sole metric of quantification.
viii) The court must be astute to ensure that a non-discloser should not be able to procure a result from his non-disclosure better than that which would be ordered if the truth were told. If the result is an order that is unfair to the non-discloser it is better that than that the court should be drawn into making an order that is unfair to the claimant.[29]

Proceeding on the basis that cryptoassets including cryptocurrencies constitute 'property' as a matter of law means that they must be disclosed in Form E (Financial Statement) in the same way as any other asset.

Most litigants will consider cryptoassets to be investments and will therefore record them in the non-exhaustive section 2.4 (Details of all investments, including shares, PEPs, ISAs, TESSAs,

26 *AB v CD* [2016] EWHC 10 (Fam) at [165].
27 As in *OG v AG* [2020] EWFC 52 at [89].
28 *Al-Khatib v Masry* [2004] EWCA Civ 1353.
29 *NG v SG* [2011] EWHC 3270 (Fam) at [16].

National Savings Investments (other than already disclosed on the form), bonds, stocks, unit trusts, investment trusts, gilts and other quoted securities that the party holds or has an interest in). Depending on how the party classifies the asset and/or its specific features, it could otherwise be disclosed in section 2.14 which includes, again non-exhaustively, unrealisable assets and the catch-all, 'any asset not disclosed elsewhere on the form even if held outside England and Wales'. The latter section reminds the party of their obligation to disclose all their financial assets and interests of any nature.

*Chapter 8*

# Practical considerations in litigation



## A. INTRODUCTION

**8.01** This chapter focuses on some of the practical issues that can arise during matrimonial finance proceedings.

In many cases, there will be an early-stage meeting with the client where they indicate that they suspect that their spouse holds, or has held, cryptoassets. Alternatively, the client may indicate that they themselves hold cryptoassets. For the former, the initial conversations will usually cover the following matters:

- Discussion of how the client knows or suspects that their partner holds cryptocurrency and whether they have corroborative evidence. Various questions can be asked, such as whether the client's partner used a cryptocurrency exchange or platform during the relationship (or to their knowledge, post-separation)? Were goods or services ever purchased by the parties using cryptocurrency? Has the client themselves been in possession of cryptocurrency and/or transferred cryptocurrency to or received cryptocurrency from their spouse? Does the client's spouse admit to owning cryptoassets, and has the client ever seen records or proof of this, such as a statement from an exchange? Does the client know which exchange(s)/platform(s) are or have been used by their spouse? Has the client and/or their spouse ever owned other digital assets, such as NFTs? If so, is there evidence of ownership of NFTs and/or any associated non-digital assets?
- Once the practitioner has gauged the degree of knowledge that the client has about their spouse's cryptocurrency holdings and the evidence that may already be available, further

lines of enquiry may be pursued. Which specific cryptocurrencies or other digital assets are held? Does the client know the quantity of the given cryptocurrency held by their partner (or, alternatively, the monetary value of the current holdings)? Critically, does the client know the type and location of the wallet(s) used by the client's spouse to hold their keys? Are the cryptoassets in question held by the client's spouse or by somebody else on their behalf? Is the client aware of any transfers of cryptocurrency to a third party (e.g. a child of the family)?

- Depending on the information and/or evidence available at this stage, it may be possible to form a tentative view as to the value of the holdings in question. The current trading price of a cryptocurrency can be accessed via online exchange websites such as Coinbase, Kraken, or Crypto.com etc. In some instances, the client's comments may be based on historic conversations or recollections with nothing recent or concrete. Given the rise and, in some cases, tremendous growth in the value of some cryptocurrencies, a modest investment years ago may now hold significant value. The opposite may of course be true, and a historic purchase of cryptocurrency may now hold little or no value. It could also be the case that a formerly-owned asset was disposed of or exchanged some time ago, or has been used to purchase another asset. Alternatively, the asset may continue to be held by the client's spouse, but its value may have been impacted by market volatility. The result is that unless the client knows the precise quantity of the asset currently held, it will often be difficult to form a preliminary view as to value without a basic level of disclosure.
- Finally, the practitioner will need to consider whether urgent steps need to be taken to obtain interim relief. Is the partner likely to deny ownership and/or attempt to dispose of their holdings in order to defeat the client's claim? Will a freezing order and/or an order to preserve relevant devices be required? Alternatively, will an application for disclosure be appropriate? Specialist advice may need to be obtained in short order.

These are some of the general points that will need to be explored at an early-stage client meeting.

## B. IDENTIFYING AND TRACING CRYPTOCURRENCY

**8.02** As suggested in Chapter 7, cryptocurrency falls to be disclosed in matrimonial finance proceedings in the same way as any other asset. What happens then if cryptoassets are not disclosed by the other side and the client knows or suspects that their spouse owns cryptoassets? What are the tell-tale signs indicating that cryptoassets are held or have been held by the counterparty?

There answer to these questions looks to how cryptocurrency is usually acquired in the first place (see Chapter 2). In summary, cryptocurrency is usually either acquired by a network participant through the process of mining, or alternatively, it is purchased. In most cases, it is likely to be the latter.

Though one cryptocurrency can be used to purchase another, as a matter of logic there will typically be an initial transaction ('on-ramping') where fiat currency such as sterling or the US dollar is deposited into an account on an exchange/trading platform and is thereafter used to purchase cryptocurrency. This may be indicated by a bank transfer or via a credit card payment, and in both instances, the transaction will be recorded as a transfer to an exchange such as Coinbase, Kraken, Crypto.com etc. on the party's bank or credit card statements. The other party's disclosure therefore needs to be reviewed carefully with this in mind.

Note, however, that the sum transferred to an exchange/trading platform may be modest, perhaps so much so that ordinarily the transaction would go unnoticed. A debit of, say, £50 to Coinbase may appear innocuous, but given the marked growth in value of some cryptocurrencies over time, that initial on-ramp transaction could represent fortuitous speculation in a now highly valuable asset. It may also be the only known transaction involving fiat currency, as thereafter any cryptocurrency purchased could be traded via the exchange. This means that finding this clue may be akin to searching for a needle in a haystack.

The elapse of time also presents a problem, as disclosure is normally limited to a short period (typically 12 months prior to Form E in the case of bank and building society statements) unless further disclosure is agreed or directed. A single and potentially low-value transfer to an exchange (which could be key evidence of the holding of cryptocurrency) could have taken place many years ago. The result is that in circumstances where the client alleges that their spouse holds cryptocurrency, an assessment will need to be made as to whether this is going to be easily proved, and indeed whether the enquiry is warranted on a costs-benefits analysis. The exercise of reviewing reams of historic statements could prove costly and disproportionate.

As considered elsewhere in this chapter, disclosure could also be sought from an exchange (*nb* the possible hurdle of obtaining trading records from entities in foreign jurisdictions) and also through expert analysis of USB drives and 'live access' to trading platforms.

If the initial question is *where do you look for evidence of cryptocurrencies?* the second question that frequently arises is *whether cryptocurrencies, and in particular, ownership of a specific holding, can be traced to and associated with a particular individual?*

Theoretically, the answer to this question is 'yes'.

One of the attractions of holding and trading with cryptocurrency is that there is a degree of privacy afforded to participants. As explained in other parts in this work, cryptocurrencies are accessed and dealt with via digital wallets that hold public and private keys. Without those keys, it is practically impossible to identify what is owned and by whom. If the individual in question has used a crypto exchange, the exchange provides them with a platform and will contain records of trades and the value of the individual's cryptocurrency holding. While users of such platforms can keep their identities hidden, they cannot hide the transactions that they have participated in. For example, in relation to Bitcoin, all transactions are public, and almost a billion transactions have already taken place. Anyone can view any of them via a block explorer.[1]

The fact that every user is anonymous presents an obvious challenge, as there is no link between a user and a transaction except a Bitcoin address (which is simply a cryptographically generated string of alphanumeric characters). Users will share this public address to receive cryptocurrencies such as Bitcoin, or they can use the private key associated with it to deal with their own holding, for example, by transferring to another individual or to pay for goods or services. As such, a bitcoin address operates as the user's pseudonym.[2]

As indicated above, the blockchain is publicly accessible, and transactions can be reviewed and monitored in real time. It is possible to view specific wallet addresses including historic transactions and current balances relating to that address. The result is that the blockchain allows transaction data to be traced through to the next address etc. but this review process is often highly technical and unlikely to be achievable for many lay persons.

If required, specialist assistance can be obtained from experts in cryptocurrency tracing and investigations such as Chainalysis, Elliptic, CipherTrace, Mitmark or Quintel.

As summarised by Chainalysis, when a Bitcoin transaction is confirmed, many details are made public automatically: the transaction hash (TxID); the sending address; the receiving address; the change address; the Unix timestamp; and the amounts sent and received.[3] While this data may be publicly available, it does not provide obvious answers when it comes to identifying the parties involved. For example, who are the pseudonymous entities? Are they cryptocurrency exchanges, merchant processors, dark net markets, or simply transacting third parties? Secondly, what is the purpose of the transaction? This could be a payment, or an investment, or a smart contract, or an attempt to transfer assets away from the holder's address. Finally, the public data does not reveal how much value is being transacted in terms of fiat currency.

It is theoretically possible to trace a specific Bitcoin or altcoin to its current location from its original address and any other addresses that it has passed through. However, this is likely to require

---

1 See, by way of example, https://www.blockchain.com/explorer.

2 A helpful blog post on this topic is available at https://blog.chainalysis.com/reports/is-bitcoin-traceable/.

3 Ibid.

expert assistance. These experts use sophisticated data collection and blockchain analytics to compare movements in public addresses and detect patterns. This means that if, for example, a party has held Bitcoin and the counterparty knows their wallet address, with specialist assistance it may be possible to determine where that Bitcoin came from, or alternatively, where it has been transferred to. If patterns can be formed, it *may* be possible to identify the relevant parties. In some cases, however, sophisticated individuals may use advanced techniques to try to evade transaction tracers, including by use of complicated 'mixers'. In those circumstances, specialist expertise will be required to trace the asset. Recourse to experts could be resource and time-intensive depending on the services required.

## C. VALUATION OF CRYPTOCURRENCY

**8.03** The starting point, and often the end point, for valuing an asset in matrimonial finance cases is that of market value. As Mostyn J put it in *FZ v SZ*, in the context of a business valuation:

> 'I have to say that simple rules are required to be applied in the vast generality of cases. This is because the family justice system depends on the majority of ancillary relief cases settling. There are enough vagaries attaching to the distributional stage of the exercise without introducing similar vagaries to the computational phase. It is hard enough for judges to advise at FDRs what the result should be without having to grapple with different measurements or concepts of value of the assets in question. If the adoption of present market value results in rough justice in some cases then that is a price worth paying in order to achieve predictability and consistency. My view is therefore that present market value should be the usual measurement of value and that fair/hope/economic values should only be used in the exceptional case. I think that serious injustice would have to be demonstrated before departure from the usual rule was justified.'[4]

For businesses, the starting point is usually to consider what a willing buyer would be prepared to pay for the business as a whole or the relevant individual's share in the business. For many partnership and sole trader businesses, save for those lacking discernible goodwill distinguishable from an individual who effectively *is* the business, the approach will usually be to value the net assets of the business before evaluating goodwill. The latter is often reflected as a multiple of annual profits or revenue. In cases involving quoted shares, the valuation will look to the price at which the shares are trading on the market, subject to specific issues such as a potential takeover or any shorting of the business. There are many authorities on business valuations that explore these issues.[5]

Cryptocurrencies such as Bitcoin are worth what they can be bought and sold for on exchanges such as Coinbase or Binance. These exchanges have websites that present current and historic

---

4 *FZ v SZ* [2010] EWHC 1630 (Fam) at [118].
5 See, eg, *Myerson v Myerson* [2009] EWCA Civ 282.

trading prices. The current value of a cryptocurrency is therefore going to be uncontroversial, and expert assistance is only likely to be required if there are significant disclosure or tracing issues.

## i. Cryptocurrency and volatility

**8.04** While the authors are anecdotally aware of many cases where the Family Court has dealt with cryptoassets, there is yet to be a Family Court authority dealing specifically with this type of asset or its valuation. As has been emphasised in other parts of this work, cryptocurrencies are often highly volatile. Volatility is a measure of how much the price of an asset moves up or down over time. Generally, the more volatile an asset is, the riskier it is seen to be as an investment. The volatility of cryptocurrency, and with it the potential for higher returns over shorter periods of time in comparison with less volatile assets, is attractive to some investors. Company shares also experience a range of volatility, but generally most shares see less dramatic upward and downward swings which take place over a longer period of time.

A cryptocurrency referred to frequently in this work, Bitcoin, has seen many volatile days since its inception. Bitcoin's all-time high on 10 November 2021 saw its value reach US$68,789.63, while its all-time low was recorded on 5 July 2013 at US$65.53. Despite its longevity, this cryptocurrency remains fundamentally volatile. On 12 May 2022, the hourly average on the high and low prices showed a 3.68% deviation in the spot market. The last time comparable numbers were recorded for Bitcoin was on 20 May 2021. According to *bitcoinist.com*, the most volatile day for Bitcoin was on 13 March 2020, where the deviation in the spot market on the hourly average touched as high as 11.91%, while on a yearly basis, 2021 was one of the most volatile years for Bitcoin, reaching highs of 6.81% deviations.[6]

Volatility, which can sometimes be extreme, is a feature of most cryptocurrencies. Ethereum is a popular cryptocurrency because of its numerous potential applications (it is currently ranked number two in the market and has seen its price increase from US$11 to over US$3,700 between 2016 to 2022). Ethereum's all-time high was on 16 November 2021 where its value reached US$4,891.70, while its all-time law was on 21 October 2015 where its value fell to the floor at US$0.4209.

This is problematic in a matrimonial finance context where it is necessary to know the value of the parties' assets. It is a point that practitioners need to be mindful of. In the case of Ethereum's price history (as of 2 June 2022), there was a seven-day high and low disparity of

---

6 https://bitcoinist.com/bitcoins-most-volatile-day-of-2022/.

US$1,721.26 / US$2,005,49. The swing was more pronounced over a 30-days (US$1,721.26 / US$2,956.69), and even more so over 90 days (US$1,721.26 / US$3,573.96). While it is possible to know the current value of a cryptocurrency by checking an exchange's website, the issue of volatility should not be overlooked. The value, say, at FDA could be very different to the value at FDR or final hearing.

Bitcoin and Ethereum are probably the two most well-known cryptocurrencies currently in circulation. Other cryptocurrencies also experience price fluctuations. Solana, for example, which is seen by some as noteworthy for its hybrid use of a 'proof-of-history' consensus mechanism, was brought to the public in 2020 and is at the time of writing ranked number nine in the market. As of 2 June 2022, it traded at US$39.73 per coin. At its all-time high on 6 November 2021, it traded at US$260.06, while its all-time low on 11 May 2020 its value was US$0.5052. At the time of writing, its seven-day high to low price swing is US$38.36 / US$48.04, Its 30-day high to low is US$38.05 / US$95.03, and its 90-day high to low is US$38.05 / US$143.02.

For newer cryptocurrencies, including those outside of the top 10 cryptocurrencies discussed in Chapter 4, the volatility may be more pronounced.

The key point to be aware of is that this asset class is typically more volatile than other familiar assets such as company shares. Fluctuations in value are not uniform across the crypto market, and the approach to valuation may depend on the specific cryptoasset involved. For example, while Bitcoin is often seen as a comparatively volatile asset, its higher trading volumes (it is by far the biggest cryptocurrency by market capitalisation) and increased institutional participation in the market has been considered by some to be reducing its volatility over time.[7] The same is not true for cryptocurrencies with lower trading volumes or up-and-coming cryptoassets like DeFi tokens which typically have a higher volatility.

## ii. Demonstrating volatility[8]

**8.05** The following charts demonstrate the fluctuating price histories of four cryptocurrencies: Bitcoin, BNB, and Ethereum, looking at each over the course of one month, three months, and one year.

---

7 Institutional clients traded US$1.14 trillion worth of cryptocurrencies on exchange Coinbase Global Inc. in 2021, up from just US$120 billion the year before, and more than twice the US$535 billion for retail: https://www.wsj.com/articles/wall-street-takes-lead-in-crypto-investments-11645927004.

8 The price history charts that follow are taken from coinmarketcap.com.

*a) Bitcoin*

**8.06**

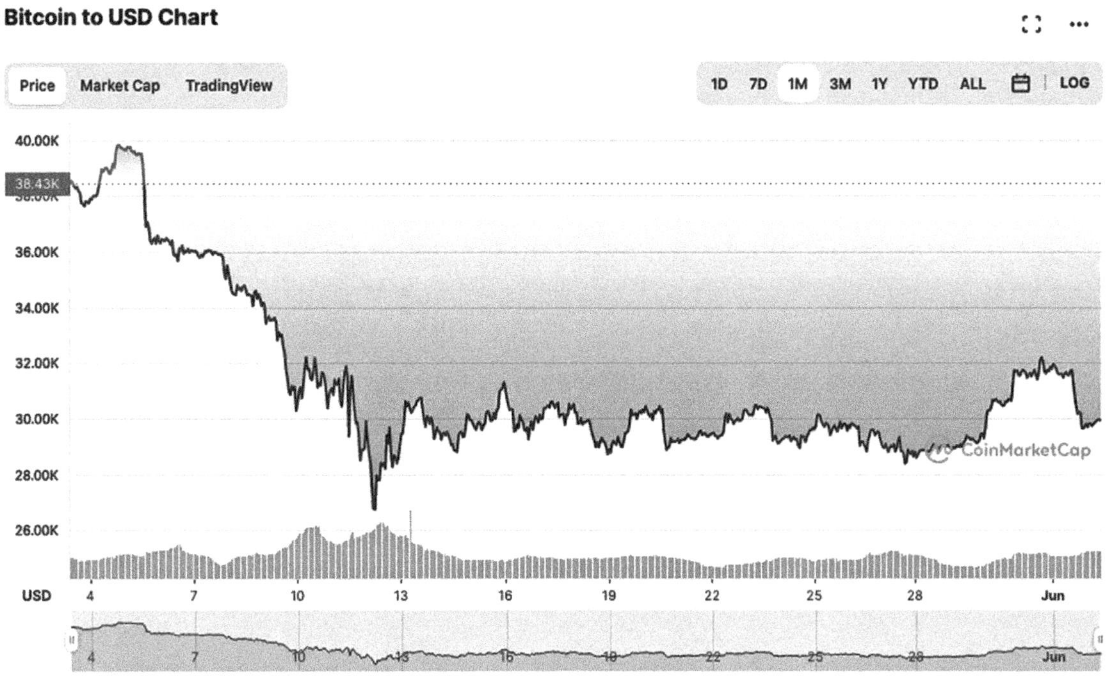


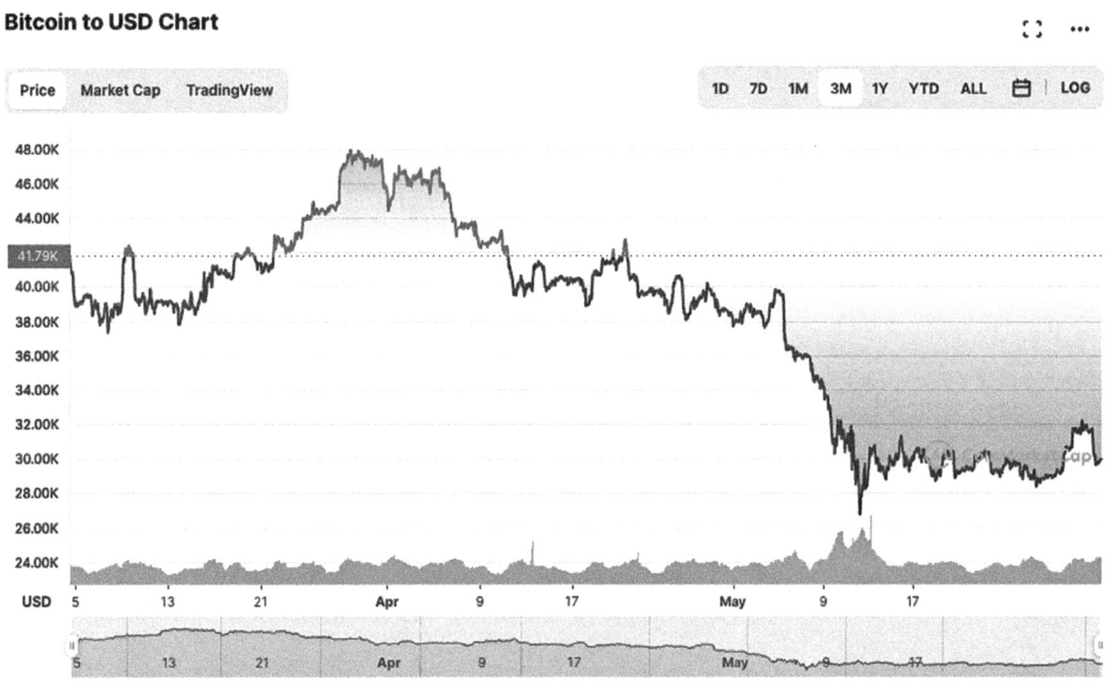

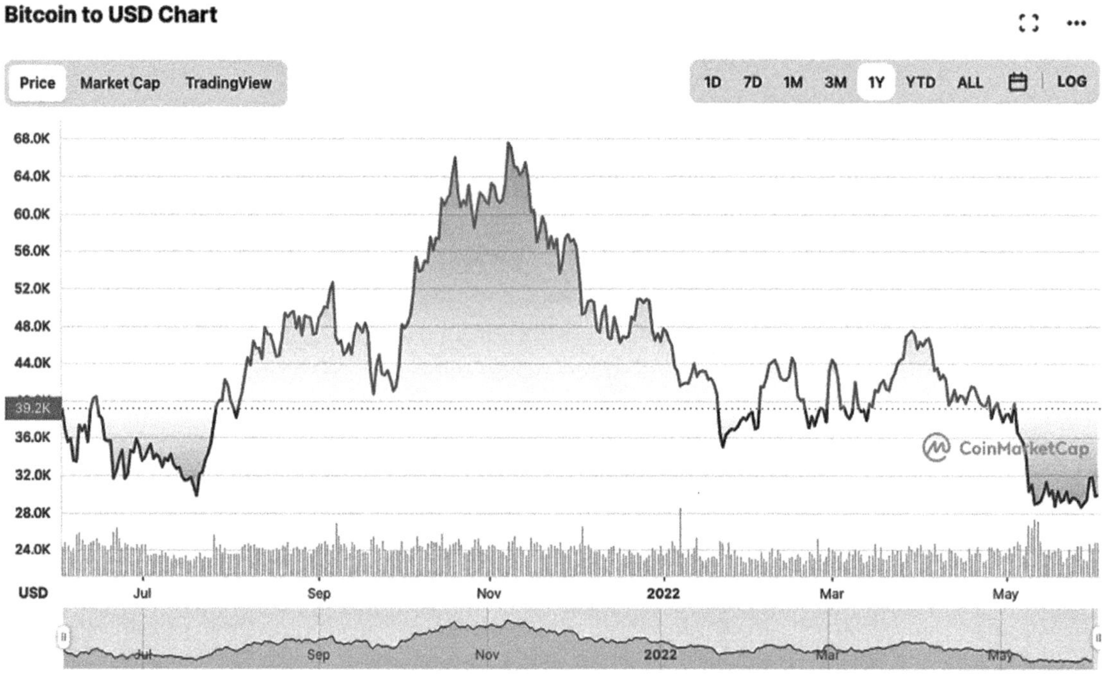
Bitcoin to USD Chart
Price
Market Cap
TradingView
1D
7D
1M
3M
1Y
YTD
ALL
LOG
68.0K
64.0K
60.0K
56.0K
52.0K
48.0K
44.0K
39.2K
36.0K
32.0K
28.0K
24.0K
USD
Jul
Sep
Nov
2022
Mar
May

*b) BNB*

**8.07**

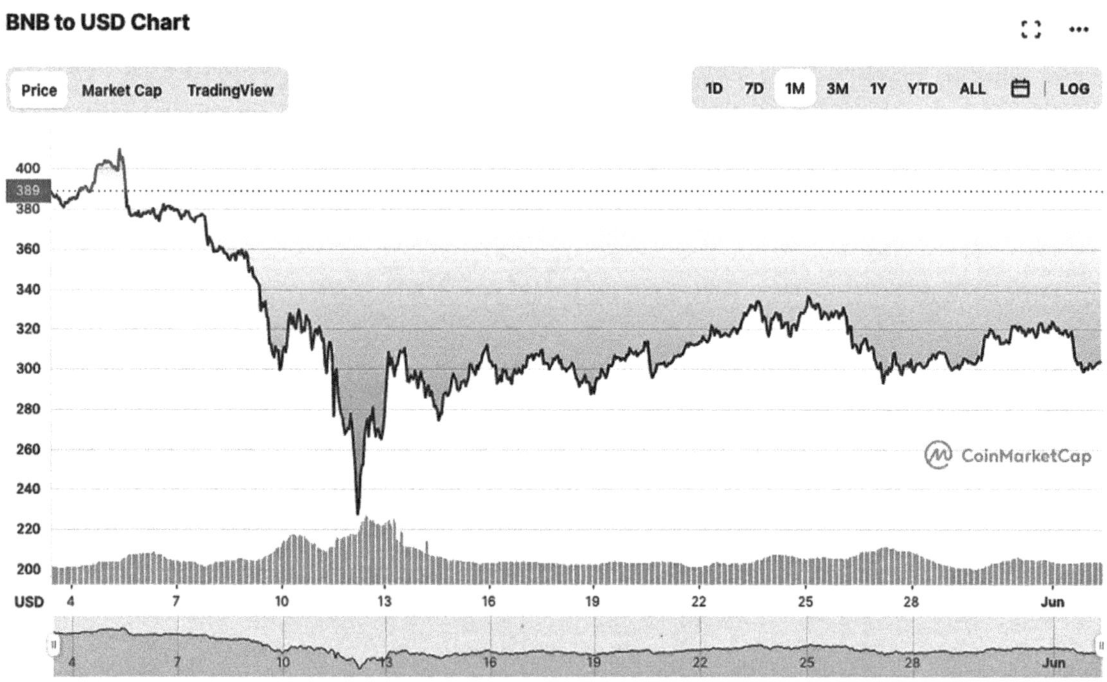
BNB to USD Chart
Price
Market Cap
TradingView
1D
7D
1M
3M
1Y
YTD
ALL
LOG
400
389
380
360
340
320
300
280
260
240
220
200
USD
4
7
10
13
16
19
22
25
28
Jun
CoinMarketCap

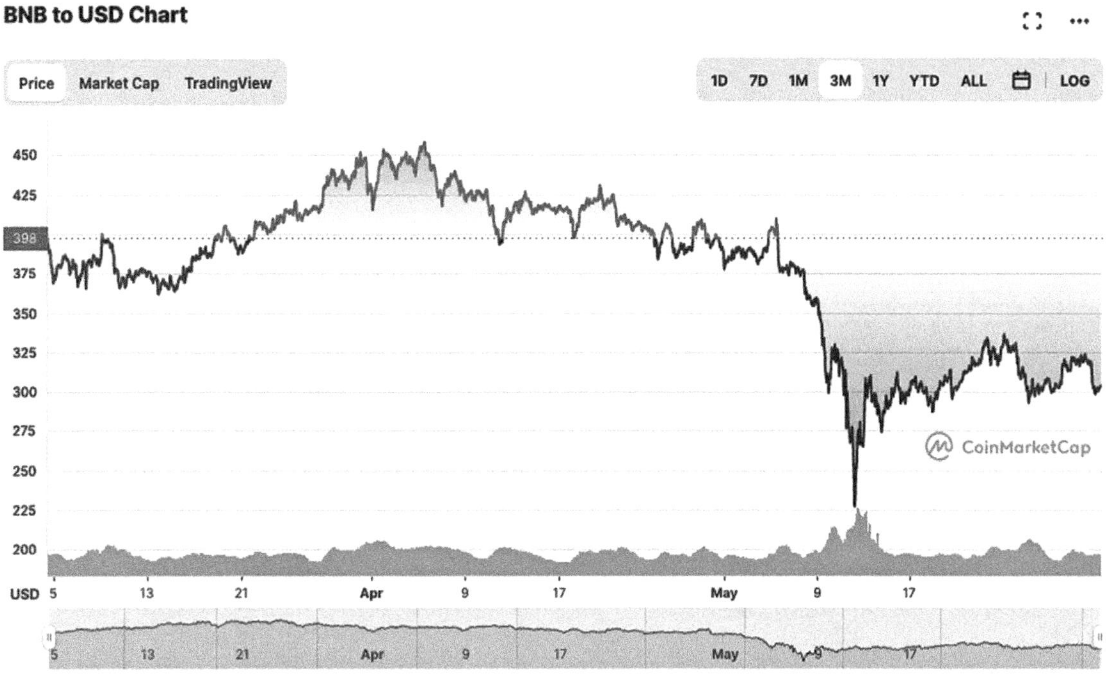
BNB to USD Chart
Price
Market Cap
TradingView
1D
7D
1M
3M
1Y
YTD
ALL
LOG
450
425
398
375
350
325
300
275
250
225
200
USD
5
13
21
Apr
9
17
May
9
17
CoinMarketCap

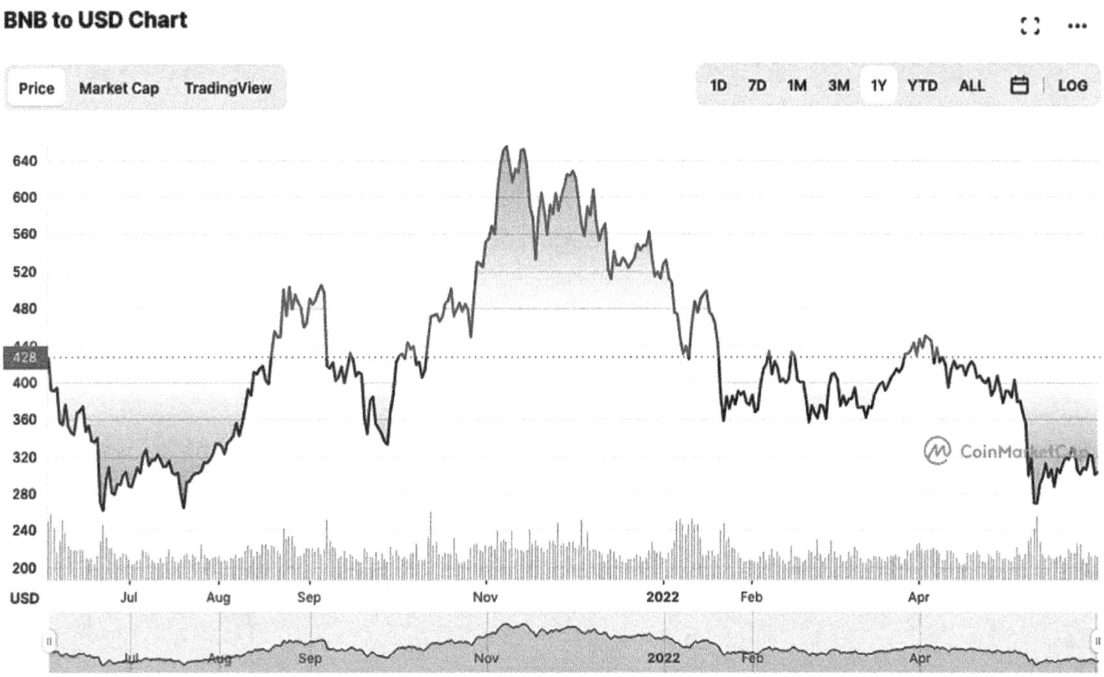
BNB to USD Chart
Price
Market Cap
TradingView
1D
7D
1M
3M
1Y
YTD
ALL
LOG
640
600
560
520
480
428
400
360
320
280
240
200
USD
Jul
Aug
Sep
Nov
2022
Feb
Apr

*c) Ethereum*

**8.08**

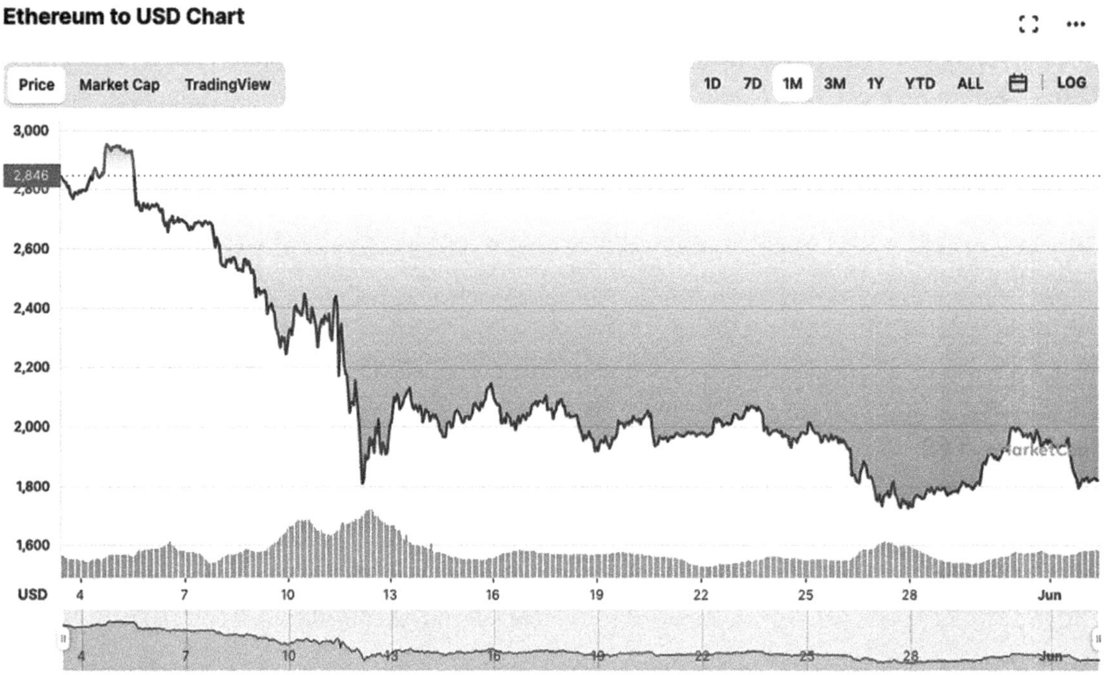


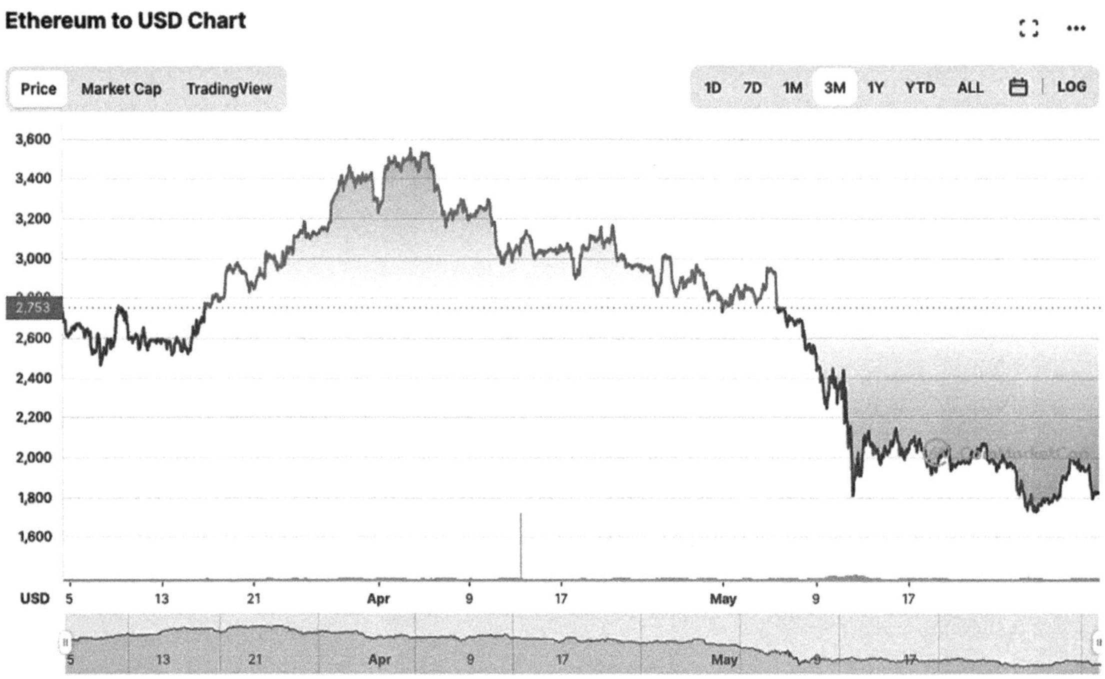

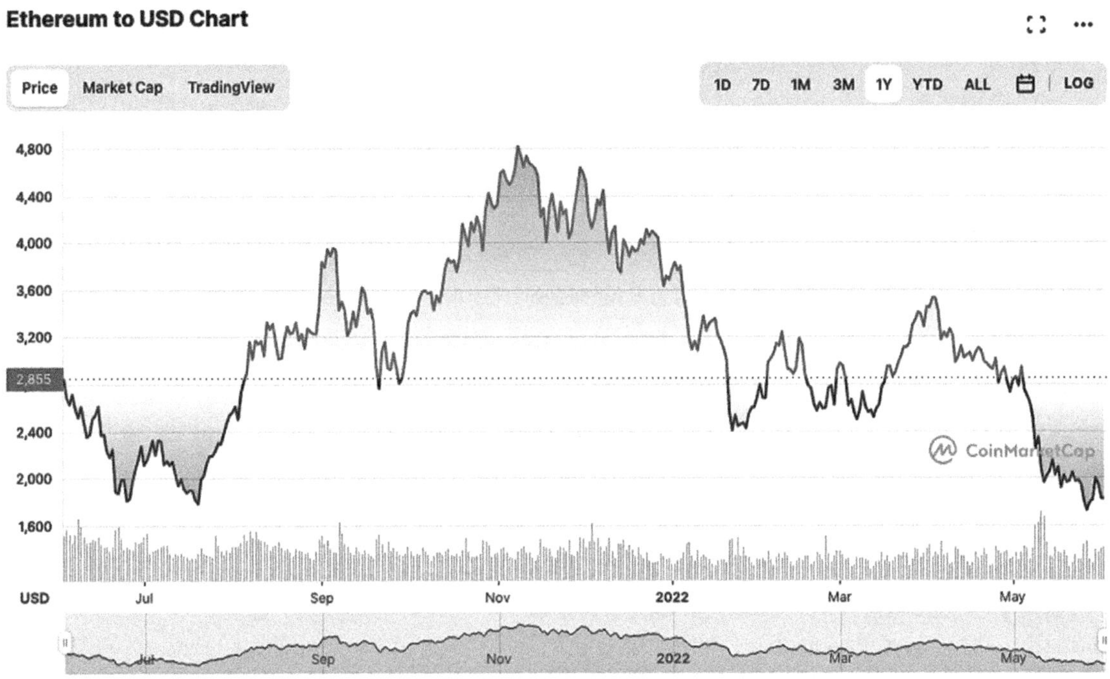


These charts show the price histories of three of the top ten cryptocurrencies by market capitalisation.

They are selected to demonstrate how prices for individual cryptocurrencies can rise and fall significantly over different periods of time. It follows that the value of a cryptocurrency at the time of Form E can change markedly during the course of the proceedings.

The charts also highlight an important point in relation to valuation methodology and timing. If, for example, the parties seek to establish an average value over time, the result may be significantly impacted by the time-range applied. As suggested above, emerging cryptocurrencies and/or those with lower trading volumes are more likely to have higher volatility over a shorter period (showing as more aggressive peaks and troughs in the data). This may impact the usefulness of an extracted average value. An alternative approach may be to obtain multiple valuations at different points in the proceedings.

### iii. What causes volatility?

**8.09** There are many reasons why cryptocurrencies may experience volatility. Supply and demand influence the prices of most commodities. By way of example, Bitcoin's market value is impacted by how many coins there are in circulation at a particular moment and what price people are willing to pay for them. A particular feature of Bitcoin is that it is limited to 21 million coins.

While this can be subdivided (see Chapter 7) as the circulating supply approaches its limit, the price *could* be impacted by scarcity.

Another factor impacting cryptocurrencies is the prospect of regulation. Any government announcement, whether in the UK or overseas, tends to have an impact on cryptocurrency prices, at least in the short term. For example,

> 'China's government and central bank announced in 2021 that all cryptocurrency transactions or facilitation were illegal. Bitcoin mining was cracked down upon following a meeting of the State Council Financial Stability and Development Committee in May, which resulted in a massive shutdown of cryptocurrency mining farms in the country. Rumours of the push to end mining in the country had caused prices to drop previously – but following the release of the committee meeting in May 2021, Bitcoin's price dropped through August 2021 to around $29,700 as miners scrambled to relocate.'[9]

Other factors that can increase volatility include positive or negative coverage in the press, as well as earnings reports. Unusually high spikes in a volume of trading typically corresponds to volatility. This is a market that is often impacted by waves of hype and speculation, which can sometimes be misplaced. For example:

> 'When media outlets announced Proshare's introduction of its Bitcoin Strategy ETF (exchange-traded fund) in late October 2021, Bitcoin's price skyrocketed over the next few weeks. Investors jumped at the chance to gain exposure to a cryptocurrency on an official exchange, causing a price jump to more than $69,000. After the hype died down and investors realized the ETF was linked to Bitcoin through futures contracts traded on the commodities market, prices dropped back down around $50,000.'[10]

Finally, as with all commodities, cryptocurrencies can be impacted by the actions of their investors. If so-called whales (investors with substantial holdings) decide to liquidate their positions in droves, that has the potential to prompt investors with more modest holdings to do the same.

### iv. Valuation and division

**8.10** The issue of volatility has been identified above. This potentially extends beyond mere fluctuations in value to the prospect of total collapse of the cryptocurrency. Most cryptocurrencies are short-lived and have little or no trading volume. Accordingly, it is of vital importance to have up-to-date valuations for any cryptocurrency holdings at every stage of the proceedings, and particularly during negotiations and for hearings. Numerous valuations may need to be obtained over the course of proceedings. Alternatively, it may be that an average value can be discerned over a specific period of time.

---

9 https://www.investopedia.com/articles/investing/052014/why-bitcoins-value-so-volatile.asp#toc-bitcoin-supply-and-demand.

10 Ibid.

A question that frequently arises is how cryptocurrencies should be treated in a settlement given the volatility issues described above. How can the court be confident of achieving a fair result when the value of an asset could change markedly from one day to the next? There is no wholly satisfactory answer to this question. As suggested above, valuations can be obtained either at a specific point or taken as an average across a specified timeframe. The parties can themselves also agree a value. As yet, there are no Family Court authorities that provide guidance on this point.

In the context of a business valuation, the Court of Appeal has observed that there is no absolute requirement for the court to attribute a specific value to an asset. In *Versteegh v Versteegh*, Singer J did not attribute a specific value to a company in circumstances where multiple experts had given incongruent valuations. The Court of Appeal upheld that approach, finding that:

> 'considerable unfairness can be caused to either, or both, parties if the approach is to be that in a sharing case, there is an absolute requirement on the court to settle on a valuation (come what may) and that, if the variables render such a valuation to be particularly friable, the court should simply adopt a conservative figure.'[11]

As was the outcome in *Versteegh*, often where the court is unable to attribute a specific value to an asset, *Wells* sharing may be appropriate.

In *Wells v Wells*, the husband at first instance retained the majority of shares in a business that was underperforming and which the court had struggled to value. The husband appealed and the Court of Appeal increased his share of the non-business assets.[12] Thorpe LJ said:

> 'In principle it seems to us that the separation of the family does not terminate the sharing of the results of the company's performance. That is easily achieved in any case in which the wife's dependency is met by continuing periodical payments. It is less easy to achieve in a clean break case. In that situation, however, sharing is achieved by a fair division of both the copper-bottomed assets and the illiquid and risk laden assets.'[13]

Accordingly, in order to achieve a fair outcome, the court may divide assets *in specie* to provide each party with a proportionate share of copper-bottomed assets as well as the illiquid or risk-laden assets. However, as was acknowledged by the Court of Appeal in *Versteegh*, 'the making of a Wells order is something that should be approached with caution by the court and against the backdrop of a full consideration by the court of its duty to consider whether it would be appropriate (per s 25A MCA 1973), to make an order which would achieve a clean

11 *Versteegh v Versteegh* [2018] EWCA Civ 1050.
12 *Wells v Wells* [2002] EWCA Civ 476.
13 At [24].

break between the parties'.[14] Of course, the value of any given cryptocurrency is available at any time on an exchange website, so the issue is not likely to be one of contested value, but rather the issue of reliance on a specific valuation given the possible risk-laden nature of the asset, particularly if it is contemplated that the cryptocurrency holdings are to be offset against a different type of asset. Given that cryptocurrencies are divisible (see Chapter 7), there is no obstruction to a clean break as there would be if spouses remain connected through joint ownership of a business.

If cryptocurrency forms a substantial part of an asset-base and there are concerns as to volatility, the courts may consider that *Wells*-style sharing produces a fairer result given that the benefit and the burden (of volatility) will be borne by both parties. It will also be open to the parties to dispose of or trade with their holding either immediately or later if that is what they wish to do. This approach may not be appropriate in all cases. Even where it is, practitioners will need to be mindful of the costs and expertise required to set up and maintain facilities to hold the cryptocurrency in question.

The question of how to attribute value to an asset was considered by Moylan LJ in *Martin v Martin* which followed shortly after *Versteegh*, again in the context of a business valuation:

> 'As referred to by both King LJ and Lewison LJ, the broad choices are (i) "fix" a value; (ii) order the asset to be sold; and (iii) divide the asset in specie: at [134] and [195]. However, to repeat, even when the court is able to fix a value this does not mean that that value has the same weight as the value of other assets such as, say, the matrimonial home. The court has to assess the weight which can be placed on the value even when using a fixed value for the purposes of determining what award to make. This applies both to the amount and to the structure of the award, issues which are interconnected, so that the overall allocation of the parties' assets by application of the sharing principle also effects a fair balance of risk and illiquidity between the parties. Again, I emphasise, this is not to mandate a particular structure but to draw attention to the need to address this issue when the court is deciding how to exercise its discretionary powers so as to achieve an outcome that is fair to both parties. I would also add that the assessment of the weight which can be placed on a valuation is not a mathematical exercise but a broad evaluative exercise to be undertaken by the judge.
>
> I would also add that this is not, as Mostyn J suggested, to take realisation difficulties into account twice. Nor, as submitted by Mr Pointer, will perceived risk always be reflected in the valuation. The need for this approach derives from the fact that, as said by Lewison LJ, there is a "difference in quality" between a value attributed to a private company and other assets. This is a relevant factor when the court is determining how to distribute the assets between the parties to achieve a fair outcome.
>
> It might be said, as Mr Marks referred to in his submissions, that it would be unfair to award one party all the "upside" in the event that the valuation proves to have been an under-estimate. That, however,

14 *Versteegh v Versteegh* [2018] EWCA Civ 1050 at [151].

is intrinsic in an asset being volatile. There is potential for the value to increase as well as decrease. If one party is not participating in that risk and is obtaining what Thorpe LJ referred to in Wells v Wells as a secure result, one aspect of achieving that result is that, because they don't have the burden of the risk of a decrease in value, they also don't have the benefit of an increase in value. As Bodey J said in Chai v Peng, at [140]. "It is a familiar approach to depart from equality of outcome where one party (usually the wife) is to receive cash, while the other party (usually the husband) is to retain the illiquid business assets with all the risks (and possible advantages) involved."'[15]

## D. DISCLOSURE, FREEZING ORDERS, AND PRESERVATION OF DEVICES

**8.11** As outlined in Chapter 3, the linking of the private key and public key allows the holder of a cryptocurrency such as Bitcoin to prove ownership and to exercise control over the asset.

The private key may be stored anywhere in a hot or cold wallet, which could be an online exchange service or else on a USB device or even a piece of paper. The private key is the 256-bit strip of alphanumeric characters that is randomly created as soon as an individual makes a wallet. Every time they deal with the asset (for example, to transfer some Bitcoin to another address, perhaps as payment for goods or services), a new private key is created for the new holder of the cryptoasset. As a result, the original key becomes redundant, and the holder of the newly created private key becomes the only person able to deal with the asset.

The important point that needs to be borne in mind is that cryptocurrency is not a physical *thing* – it is data. The ability to access and control that data is the only way to access and control the asset itself.

If, for example, a private key is lost and cannot be found, whether innocently or not, there will be no way to access the cryptocurrency. To emphasise the point, a recent cautionary tale came in 2021 where it was reported that a man in Newport, Wales had thrown away an old PC hard drive in 2013 and had spent eight years looking for it. Little did he know at the time, but the hard drive contained a wallet with 7,500 Bitcoin (now worth some US$350 million).[16] To date it has not been found.

The fact that cryptocurrencies exist in a financial system without any centralised government or financial institution controlling its operation means that there can be practical difficulties when it comes to preserving and/or enforcing against the asset. Without a centralised authority, a

15 *Martin v Martin* [2018] EWCA Civ 2866 at [92]–[98].

16 https://www.iflscience.com/technology/man-searches-through-landfill-for-8-years-for-350-million-lost-bitcoin-wallet/.

freezing injunction could be pointless if there is no third party to serve, even where the assets are identified (cf the position with a conventional freezing order involving bank accounts). This in all likelihood means that only an *in personam* order is going to be effective. Another by-product of decentralisation is the fact that there is no easy way to obtain confirmed information from a third-party about an individual's holdings. Moreover, if, for example, cryptocurrency has been transferred from a party to an unknown recipient, a practitioner may need to consider the efficacy of obtaining a freezing order against 'persons unknown'.

## i. Questionnaires

**8.12** As with all varieties of asset, ownership of cryptocurrency will fall within the scope of a party's ongoing duty to provide full, frank, and clear disclosure. In many cases they will be properly disclosed, whether in voluntary disclosure or on Form E (most likely, in sections 2.4 or 2.14). In those circumstances, practitioners will need to consider what questions may need to be asked in a questionnaire when cryptoassets are disclosed and what evidence should be sought in the first instance if it has not already been provided. In the absence of a Family Court authority, or a reference to cryptoassets on Form E, there is no standard level of disclosure or specimen questions in common circulation.

The following questions are therefore presented as a starting point for consideration.[17] They will need to be amended to fit the circumstances of the case. The drafting will reflect, for example, the extent to which the assets are meaningful in value, and/or whether there is suspected non-disclosure or dissipation of the cryptoassets. If, for example, the cryptoassets are comparatively modest in value, many of the following questions will not be appropriate.

As with all questions and requests for documents, proportionality will need to be at the forefront of the practitioner's mind. As suggested above, gathering the evidence and reviewing replies may prove costly and time intensive. Expert assistance may also be required which carries further costs implications. As with all questions, they may need to be justified before the court.

Example questions:

- Please provide details of [and disclose the public key for] all cryptocurrency wallets or accounts (whether with a cryptocurrency exchange or wallet provider or otherwise) of any kind that you have owned or have had an interest in (whether in your own name or jointly with other persons, and whether or not in your control), from [DATE] to present.

17 With grateful thanks to Andrzej Bojarski (36 Family) for his contributions to the specimen questions.

- Please provide a schedule setting out all cryptocurrencies you have purchased, sold, or transacted with from [DATE] to present, with documentary evidence in support confirming the amount and dates of all such transactions, and stating in each case the cryptocurrency wallets or accounts (whether with a cryptocurrency exchange or wallet provider or otherwise) into which the cryptocurrencies were received or from which they were transferred.
- Please confirm the source of funds (including, where appropriate, identification of any relevant bank account or credit card or loan facilities, with copies of relevant statements) for all purchases of cryptocurrencies [above [VALUE]] from [DATE] to present.
- Please confirm the receipt of funds from all sale, transfer or disposal of cryptocurrencies [above [VALUE]] from [DATE] to present (including, where appropriate, identification of any relevant bank account or other account into which the proceeds of sale, transfer or disposal was paid, with copies of relevant statements).
- Please provide documentary evidence of the current holdings of all cryptocurrencies held in each wallet, exchange, or other cryptocurrency account held by you (whether held in your own name or jointly with other persons, or by any person as your nominee, trustee, or custodian). In the event any such information or documentation is not within your personal custody or control please identify the person who has such information and provide their address and contact details.
- Please provide statements showing all transactions involving cryptocurrencies owned and/or controlled by you from [DATE] to present.
- [Please provide bank or credit card statements that identify all transactions to or from any cryptocurrency wallet, exchange, or other cryptocurrency account of any description owned or controlled by you from [DATE] to present.]

## ii. Freezing orders

**8.13** Pursuant to section 37(2)(a) of the Matrimonial Clauses Act 1973 (MCA 1973), where the court is satisfied that a party is about to make a disposition with the intention of defeating a claim for financial relief, it may make an order restraining him or her from proceeding. The required intention is presumed if the effect of an intended disposition would be to defeat the applicant's claim. There will, however, need to be a finding of fact as to relevant intention.[18] The Family Court also has inherent jurisdiction pursuant to section 37 Senior Courts Act 1981 and Family Procedure Rule 20.2 to order a freezing injunction restraining a party from disposing of assets.

The strict conditions to be fulfilled before a freezing order is granted are well-known. The adverse consequences of non-compliance with those principles were warned by Mostyn J

[18] *DW v Anor v CG* [2016] EWHC 2965 (Fam).

in *UL v BK*.[19] In that case Mostyn J returned to the principles governing a freezing application made under section 37 Senior Courts Act 1981 and considered whether there is a difference in the test to be applied under section 37 MCA 1973:

> '17. [...] it is convenient to return to the principles which govern a freezing application made under s37 of the 1981 Act. I attempted to set them out in ND v KP. Put shortly, those principles, as summarised in the White Book, require an applicant to put forward an appropriately strong case, supported by evidence of objective facts (rather than mere expressions of suspicion or anxiety), that the respondent owned or had an interest in specified assets and that there was a real risk of their dissipation.
>
> 18. It seems to me that prima facie proof of a risk of dissipation requires, at least in general and broad terms, proof of an intention to dissipate – dissipation in this context surely means a deliberate or reckless dealing with assets rather than some random event unconnected to the motives of the respondent. I acknowledge that in Alternative Investment Solutions (General) Ltd v Valle de Uco Resort and Spa SA [2013] EWHC 333 (QB) at para 8 Cranston J stated: "There is no need for a claimant to show an intention to dissipate assets, nor dishonesty or fraud. Where there is a good arguable case of dishonesty or fraud the risk of dissipation may speak for itself. The conduct giving rise to a real risk of dissipation must not be capable of justification". This would suggest that proof of a nefarious intent is not needed, but that proof of unjustified conduct will suffice. I consider that there is no real difference between the two. It may be that Cranston J was drawing a distinction between express and inferred intentions. In my opinion if someone is doing something unjustified with his assets then it surely follows as night follows day that he must (in a non-innocent way) be intending to do so.
>
> 19. In my judgment it is therefore a fallacy to suggest that under s37 of the 1973 Act proof of intention is required whereas under s37 of the 1981 Act it is not. Under both procedures an unjustified dealing with assets will likely supply prima facie proof of an intention to dissipate. And, of course, under s37(5)(b) Matrimonial Causes Act 1973 the intention to defeat the applicant's claim is presumed in the case of an immediately prospectant transaction. This would suggest that, if anything, it is in fact easier to obtain the injunction under s37 Matrimonial Causes Act 1973 than under the 1981 counterpart because under the former all the applicant has to show is that a transaction is about to happen which would have the effect, if not restrained, of defeating her claim, while under the former there has to be shown by her some unjustified dealing by the respondent with assets giving rise to a risk of dissipation. But I repeat that I do not believe that there is in fact any real difference between the two tests.'

Accordingly, there needs to be solid evidence of the respondent's intention to dissipate assets. The applicant needs to have a good arguable case and persuade a court that refusal of the relief sought would involve a real risk of injustice. The relevant principles and safeguards were summarised (at [51]) as follows:

> '1. The court has a general power to preserve specific tangible assets in specie where they are the subject matter of the claim. Such an order does not necessarily require application of all the freezing order principles and safeguards, although it is open to the court to impose them.

[19] *UL v BK* [2013] EWHC 1735 (Fam).

2. For a freezing order in a sum of money which is capable of embracing all of the respondent's assets up to the specified figure it is essential that all the principles and safeguards are scrupulously applied.
3. Whether the application is made under the 1981 Act or the 1973 Act the applicant must show, by reference to clear evidence, an unjustified dealing with assets (which would include threats) by the respondent giving rise to the conclusion that there is a solid risk of dissipation of assets to the applicant's prejudice. Such an unjustified dealing will normally give rise to the inference that it is done with the intention to defeat the applicant's claim (and such an intention is presumed in the case of an application under the 1973 Act).
4. The evidence in support of the application must depose to clear facts. The sources of information and belief must be clearly set out.
5. Where the application for a freezing order is made ex parte the applicant has to show that the matter is one of exceptional urgency. Short informal notice must be given to the respondent unless it is essential that he is not made aware of the application. No notice at all would only be justified where there is powerful evidence that the giving of any notice would likely lead the respondent to take steps to defeat the purpose of the injunction, or where there is literally no time to give any notice before the order is required to prevent the threatened wrongful act. Cases where no notice at all can be justified are very rare indeed. The order of the court should record on its face the reason why it was satisfied that no or short notice was given.
6. Where no notice, or short informal notice, is given the applicant is fixed with a high duty of candour. Breach of that duty will likely lead to a discharge of the order. The applicable principles on the re-grant of the order after discharge are set out in Arena Corporation v Schroeder at para 213.
7. Where no notice, or short informal notice, is given the safeguards assume critical importance. The safeguards are set out in the standard examples for freezing and search orders. If an applicant seeks to dis-apply any safeguard the court must be made unambiguously aware of this and the departure must be clearly justified. The giving of an undertaking in damages, whether to the respondent or to an affected third party, is an almost invariable requirement; release of this must be clearly justified.'

As with all freezing orders, the applicant must be scrupulously candid if the application is made *ex parte*. This will often be the case with applications concerning cryptocurrency given the speed with which they can potentially be dissipated. Material non-disclosure is likely to result in the order being discharged with indemnity costs being ordered against the applicant. Mostyn J has said, by way of warning (at [52]) that:

> 'It is worth remembering not only that the ex parte procedure is intrinsically unfair but also, and very importantly, that a case which begins with an ex parte order is usually poisoned from that point onwards. The unilateral step taken at the beginning of case echoes down its history. Often the respondent is enraged by the step taken against him and looks to take counter-offensive measures. Every single subsequent step is coloured by that fateful first step. Costs tend to mount exponentially. And even after the lawyers close their files and render their final bills the personal relations of the spouses will likely remain forever soured. A nuclear winter often ensues. This is not to say that sometimes, but very rarely, an ex parte application is necessary. Insistence on the imposition of the stringent conditions and detailed

> safeguards might have the side-effect of mitigating the unhappy consequences to which I have referred. In B v A [2012] EWHC 3127 (Fam) Charles J dealt with an (alleged) child abduction case, where there had been flagrant disregard of the established principles. In para 110 he stated:
>
> > "It seems to me that if such failures are to be avoided in the future there is a need for judges:
> >
> > (i) to refuse to make without notice orders if the established principles and procedures are not applied (I and some other judges do this), and
> >
> > (ii) to treat such failures as negligent and thus as a foundation for the exercise of discretion to make a wasted costs order."'
>
> In that case a wasted costs order in the sum of £18,000 was made against the applicant's solicitors. It must be expected that future abuse of the principles may lead to similar orders being made in the future.'

In that decision, Mostyn J also confirmed that in respect of draft orders for freezing injunctions that he agreed with the comment in the *White Book* at 25.1.25.6 that 'any departure from the standard wording must be drawn to the attention of the judge hearing the without notice application'. It is the authors' view that various amendments to the standard precedent for a freezing order contained in the suite of family orders (Order 3.1) will be required and these should be highlighted to the court. The precise amendments will need to reflect the circumstances of the case.

The effectiveness of any freezing order may depend on whether the target assets are held on an exchange (which can be served with the order and may or may not be located in this jurisdiction) or on some form of non-custodial wallet. If the cryptocurrency in question is held in a non-custodial wallet, then it will fall to the respondent or other individual with control of the wallet to comply with the order's terms.

The following observations are made as to the drafting of such orders where the objective is to secure cryptocurrency. Advice may need to be taken to ensure that the drafting meets the requirements of the case.

- Care should be taken over the definition of 'cryptocurrency' or 'cryptoasset'. The chosen term should be purposefully broad as well as specifying, where appropriate, the specific cryptocurrencies in question (eg Bitcoin, Solana, Ethereum etc). Likewise, the order will need to include comprehensive definitions of terms such as 'private key', 'wallet' and 'exchange' (as appropriate).
- The usual undertaking for damages may require a carve-out stating that the applicant will not be responsible for loss occasioned by fluctuations in market value or exchange rates.
- The terms of the operative paragraphs of the injunction will need to reflect the circumstances of the case. They could prevent the respondent from taking some or all of the following steps:
  1. use or amendment/variation of any private key in the respondent's possession or [direct or indirect] control;

ii. transfer or disclosure of any private key in the respondent's possession or [direct or indirect] control to any third party, whether an individual or entity;
iii. restriction of access to any accounts in the respondent's name (or accounts over which the respondent has or can gain access to) with a cryptocurrency exchange (as defined) for any purpose;
iv. transfer or removal or dealing with any cryptocurrency wallet (as defined), including but not limited to the transfer or removal of the same outside of the jurisdiction;
v. perform any action or take any step that would or could cause the cryptocurrency (as defined) to fall in value or be disposed of or be transferred to any other location or person or entity, or in any way to deal with the cryptocurrency.

- The suggestions above reflect the fact that simply referring to, say, the freezing of a specific quantity of Bitcoin is unlikely to suffice on its own. As explained above, the private key controls the asset and therefore both the private key and the wallet containing it need to be addressed in the order. It is important to prevent the use or disclosure of the private key. This means that if the private key is known to be contained on any USB device or computer or other device, that will also need to be reflected in the order and preserved accordingly. Thought should be given as to whether any third parties are aware of or have a copy of the private key, noting that they can be held in duplicate.
- In a case where the cryptocurrency or the private key is stored in a hot or cold wallet or on an exchange outside of the jurisdiction, it will be necessary to prohibit dealing with the same or changing their location. By definition, cryptocurrency is not located in a single jurisdiction (its very nature is that it is decentralised), which means that the focus is going to be on the location of the wallet containing the private key. This may require drafting that prevents any physical device from leaving the jurisdiction and/or restricting the online transfer of the private key to an exchange or other online service provider located outside of England and Wales. As always, the drafting will need to reflect the circumstances of the case.
- In cases where a party has already dissipated the asset it may be difficult to identify the new holder(s) of the cryptocurrency. In those circumstances, as discussed in Chapter 7, the court may make an order against 'persons unknown'. Such an order is, however, unusual in the context of family proceedings but may be required if the evidence available suggests that the respondent has an interest in the asset which is held or controlled by another person whose identity is unknown.

## iii. Disclosure and preservation of devices

**8.14** The parties to matrimonial proceedings are under an ongoing duty to provide full, frank, and clear disclosure of their finances.[20] That duty subsists from the point of Form E onwards

[20] *US v SR* [2014] EWHC 175 (Fam).

until the final order is sealed.[21] Mostyn J outlined the impact of materially deficient disclosure in *NG v SG (Appeal: Non-Disclosure)*:[22]

> 'Pulling the threads together it seems to me that where the court is satisfied that the disclosure given by one party has been materially deficient then:
>
> i) The Court is duty bound to consider by the process of drawing adverse inferences whether funds have been hidden.
>
> ii) But such inferences must be properly drawn and reasonable. It would be wrong to draw inferences that a party has assets which, on an assessment of the evidence, the Court is satisfied he has not got.
>
> iii) If the Court concludes that funds have been hidden then it should attempt a realistic and reasonable quantification of those funds, even in the broadest terms.
>
> iv) In making its judgment as to quantification the Court will first look to direct evidence such as documentation and observations made by the other party.
>
> v) The Court will then look to the scale of business activities and at lifestyle.
>
> vi) Vague evidence of reputation or the opinions or beliefs of third parties is inadmissible in the exercise.
>
> vii) The Al-Khatib v Masry technique of concluding that the non-discloser must have assets of at least twice what the Claimant is seeking should not be used as the sole metric of quantification.
>
> viii) The Court must be astute to ensure that a non-discloser should not be able to procure a result from his non-disclosure better than that which would be ordered if the truth were told. If the result is an order that is unfair to the non-discloser it is better that than that the Court should be drawn into making an order that is unfair to the Claimant.'

The need to address inadequate disclosure may run in tandem with an urgent need to preserve devices or documents that contain keys. The reason for this has been emphasised at many points in this work: control of the private key provides control of the asset. Commentary on the contents of a Questionnaire where cryptocurrency has been disclosed is set out above.

In situations where the location of the keys is unknown, an order for providing for the preservation of documents, the private key, and any relevant devices may be appropriate. What the order will specifically cover will reflect the circumstances of the case, but as a general matter the following observations are made:

- Thought needs to be given to the defined terms used in the order. It will usually be beneficial to have as comprehensive a definition of 'cryptocurrency' as possible, which may include reference to specific contemplated cryptocurrencies. Depending on the case, it may be that the term 'cryptoasset' is appropriate if the contemplated assets go beyond the conventional definition of 'cryptocurrency'. Likewise, the definitions of 'document' and 'device' should be carefully

21 *N v N* [2014] EWCA Civ 314.
22 *NG v SG (Appeal: Non-Disclosure)* [2011] EWHC 3270 at [16].

drafted, noting that private keys can be held on any combination of hot or cold wallets, which can include a physical location (eg a paper document) or device (eg a USB drive) or on an online wallet hosting service or trading platform.

- Where the location of the keys is unknown, it may be necessary to prohibit the respondent from taking any steps to amend, damage, erase, or in any way deal with or alter any information or data (howsoever construed) held on any document or device or online storage location (all as defined) that are within their possession or direct or indirect control. Further wording could be inserted to prevent the means of storage of the keys (whatever that may be) from being removed from the jurisdiction.
- The respondent will usually need to be prohibited from accessing any online exchange or trading platform or wallet hosting service, and from using any key for any purpose.
- The preservation order should also prohibit disclosure of any keys within the respondent's possession or knowledge or direct or indirect control to any third party, whether a person or entity.
- In situations where a key is known to already be in the possession of a third party, the draft order could prohibit that party (who would need to be a respondent and could potentially be 'Persons Unknown') from disclosing or delivering any of the aforementioned means of storage to the first respondent or any other person.
- Where the client knows that specific devices have been used to store keys or information relating to cryptoasset holdings, a specific document and device preservation order could be sought in conjunction with an order for delivery up of those documents or devices.
- Finally, in circumstances where the location of the means of storage of the keys is unknown (and even where it is), it may be beneficial to seek an order for specific disclosure, the fruits of which can be provided to the applicant and/or any expert that may have been appointed. The specific disclosure order will, like the other orders mentioned above, need to be drafted to accommodate the objectives of the application and the circumstances of the case. The following information could be requested:

  i. Full details of any cryptocurrencies (or cryptoassets) held or which have been held over a specified period.
  ii. Full details of all keys (private and public) relating to cryptocurrencies (or cryptoassets) held by the respondent or over which the respondent has had access or control over a specified period.
  iii. Details of any means of storage (and locations) where keys for any cryptocurrencies (or cryptoassets) may be held. It may also be appropriate to obtain any relevant addresses, log-in details, passwords, or other information required to access those means of storage.
  iv. Details of any other devices or means/methods of storage of keys that the respondent has used but which are no longer in use or in their possession or control, along with details of when they were last within their possession or control and where they are located now. Note that control can be direct or indirect.

v. The expert may require log-in details and passwords for all exchanges/trading platforms used by the respondent. The respondent could also be required, if necessary, to attend at the expert's offices or such other location as would be specified by the expert in order to facilitate access to the account(s).

vi. If necessary, the order could provide for delivery up of any devices, documents or physical means or storage for analysis by the expert. This could include, for example, desktop computers, USB drives etc.

Thought will need to be given as to whether disclosure of the private key is actually necessary or appropriate in the circumstances, given that knowledge of the private key bestows control of the asset. This will carry with it a risk that the assets are improperly accessed or lost.

Practitioners may also wish to consider the efficacy of a search order. Pursuant to Family Procedure Rule 20.2(1), the court is empowered to make an order providing for the detention, custody or preservation of property, which includes documents. The procedure relating to search orders is set out in paragraph 6.1 of Family Procedure Rules PD20A. They are comparatively rare in family proceedings.

In summary, when applying for a search order, a supervising solicitor is appointed (a solicitor that must be experienced in the operation of such orders). An *ex parte* application is then made, supported by an affidavit giving full details of the supervising solicitor and the address of the premises to be searched and setting out fully the reasons why the order is sought, including the probability that documents may disappear if the order were not made.

The order, if obtained, must be served personally by the supervising solicitor, together with the evidence in support, unless the court orders otherwise. There are detailed rules about how service is to be conducted, as well as the search and custody of materials (paragraphs 6.4–6.5).

## E. 'SELF-HELP' DISCLOSURE AND ASSOCIATED CRIMINAL OFFENCES

**8.15** Cryptoassets fall to be disclosed within matrimonial finance proceedings in same way as any other asset.

A by-product of how information and records relating to cryptocurrency holdings are typically held (frequently online and/or within electronic devices) as well as the frequent paucity of evidence of the same, means that practitioners must be particularly alert to the dangers of so-called 'self-help' disclosure and associated offences under the Computer Misuse Act 1990 ('CMA 1990') and the Data Protection Act 2018 ('DPA 2018') when this type of asset features in a case. This section provides an outline of the current law relating to the interception of documents belonging to the other party and also the aforementioned legislation.

The position relating to 'self-help' changed significantly in light of the Court of Appeal's decision in *Tchenguiz & Ors v Imerman*.[23] This brought to an end the practice that had arisen following the decision in *Hildebrand v Hildebrand* (ie that it was common practice to take copies of the other party's documents for use in the litigation, provided that it was not obtained by force or trespass, on the basis that the originals must be returned to the owner and they should be promptly notified of any documents that had been taken).[24] In *Imerman*, the Court of Appeal held that 'the so-called *Hildebrand* rules' were not authority for that practice. *Hildebrand* was in fact only authority 'as to the time when copies obtained unlawfully or clandestinely should be disclosed to a spouse'. Given that *Hildebrand* is no longer justifiable as a practice, it follows that practitioners need to act with extreme caution in circumstances where a client improperly obtains documents.

The key points coming out of *Imerman* are as follows:

- As to the question of whether the courts are to condone the illegality of self-help consisting of breach of confidence (or tort), because it is feared that the other side will itself behave unlawfully and conceal that which should be disclosed, the answer could only be 'no' [107].
- Nothing in the so-called Hildebrand rules can be relied upon in justification of, or as providing a defence to, conduct which would otherwise be criminal or actionable (whether as a tort or in equity) nor as providing any reason why the relief (whether at law or in equity) which would otherwise be available should not be granted [121].
- 'Communications which are concerned with an individual's private life, including his personal finances, personal business dealings, and (possibly) his other business dealings are the stuff of personal confidentiality, and are specifically covered by article 8 of the Convention, which confers the right to respect for privacy and expressly mentions correspondence' [76]. Note, however, that: 'if a husband leaves his bank statement lying around open in the matrimonial home, in the kitchen, living room or marital bedroom, it may well lose its confidential character as against his wife. The court may have to consider the nature of the relationship and the way the parties lived, and conducted their personal and business affairs. Thus, if the parties each had their own study, it would be less likely that the wife could copy the statement without infringing the husband's confidence if it had been left by him in his study rather than in the marital bedroom, and the wife's case would be weaker if the statement was kept in a drawer in his desk and weaker still if kept locked in his desk. But, as we have already said, confidentiality is not dependent upon locks and keys. Thus the wife might well be able to maintain, as against her husband, the confidentiality of her personal diary or journal, even though it was kept visible and unlocked on her dressing table'. [88].

23 *Tchenguiz & Ors v Imerman* [2010] 2 FLR 814.
24 *Hildebrand v Hildebrand* [1992] 1 FLR 244.

- The relationship between the parties and the circumstances in which the information or document is obtained is relevant only to the question as to whether the information or document is to be cloaked with confidentiality. Once it is determined that the document is properly to be regarded as confidential to one spouse but not to the other, the relationship has no further relevance in relation to the remedy for breach of that confidentiality [89].
- The rules only require a party to give full disclosure under Form E. Only thereafter might a party be ordered to disclose further documents should the court think it necessary [140].
- Where a party is likely to suppress documents and there 'exists evidence of an intention to salt away assets to as to deceive the court', the remedies look to the court's powers to grant search and seize, freezing, preservation, and other similar orders, to ensure that assets are not wrongly concealed or dissipated, and that evidence is not wrongly destroyed or concealed [128]. However, the Court of Appeal noted the decision in *Burgess v Burgess*[25] where Waite LJ suggested that a search and seize order was 'a rare weapon for use only in extreme or exceptional cases'. In reply, the decision in *Imerman* held that: 'If (as we believe) Waite LJ thereby meant that such an order would rarely be sought in ancillary relief proceedings and should only be sought when it was proportionate, just as in proceedings in the Queen's Bench and Chancery Divisions, then we would agree. However, if (which we doubt) he meant that such orders should be more difficult to obtain in ancillary relief proceedings than in ordinary civil proceedings, we would disagree.' [133].
- In terms of the question of whether the court can admit evidence in matrimonial finance proceedings that has been improperly obtained: 'while the court can admit such evidence, it has power to exclude it if unlawfully obtained, including power to exclude documents whose existence has only been established by unlawful means. In exercising that power, the court will be guided by what is "necessary for disposing fairly of the application for ancillary relief or for saving costs", and will take into account the importance of the evidence, "the conduct of the parties", and any other relevant factors, including the normal case management aspects. Ultimately, this requires the court to carry out a balancing exercise, something which, we are well aware, is easy to say in general terms but is often very difficult to effect in individual cases in practice' [177]. However, note that the court may take a rigorous position on this if there is the possibility of unfairness to the disclosing party.[26]
- The Court of Appeal also addressed the risk of solicitors being sued for damages: 'In this connection, we were taken to the observation of Eady J in White v Withers LLP [2008] EWHC 2821 (QB), para [8], that "the mere receipt of documents by the solicitors from their client and their continued retention in connection with the matrimonial proceedings simply cannot give rise to a cause of action". In our view, that observation (which may in any event have been limited to a cause of action in damages) should be taken as applying only to the receipt

25 *Burgess v Burgess* [1996] 2 FLR 34.
26 See, eg *Arbili v Arbili* [2015] EWCA Civ 542.

of documents by solicitors from their client; further, it should not be taken as suggesting that the claimant could not recover the documents from the solicitors.' [70]

The manner in which documents that have been improperly obtained should be dealt with was summarised by Mostyn J in *UL v BK (Freezing Orders: Safeguards: Standard Examples)*:[27]

'i) Whatever the historic practice (and however alluring the arguments for pragmatism and practicality) it is simply and categorically unlawful for a wife (for it usually is she) to breach her husband's privacy by furtively copying his documents whether they exist in hard copy or electronically. There may be factual issues about whether the documents are actually in the husband's private domain; but if they are (and they almost always are) then it is wholly impermissible for the wife to access and copy them.

ii) If a wife does access such private documents she is not only in jeopardy of criminal penalties but also risks being civilly sued by the husband for breach of confidence and misuse of his private material.

iii) If a wife supplies such documents to her solicitor then the solicitor must not read them but must immediately seek to obtain all of them from the wife and must return them, and all copies (both hard and soft), to the husband's solicitor (if he has one). The husband's solicitor, who owes a high duty to the court, will read them and disclose those of them that are both admissible and relevant to the wife's claim, pursuant to the husband's duty of full and frank disclosure. If before that exercise has taken place the husband's solicitor is dis-instructed the solicitor must retain those documents pending a further order of the court.

iv) If the husband does not have a solicitor the wife's solicitor must retain the documents, unread, and in sealed files, and must approach the court for directions. Those directions will likely be to the effect that the wife shall pay for an independent lawyer to be instructed to determine which of those documents are admissible and relevant to the wife's claim. Copies can then be provided to the wife's solicitor before the files of documents are returned to the husband.

v) The wife is permitted to rely on her knowledge of the documents to challenge the veracity of the husband's disclosure in the proceedings. Her knowledge is admissible evidence. For this purpose she can express her recollection to her solicitor, and the solicitor can advise on it. However, if the expression of that recollection involves the revelation of clearly privileged matters then the solicitor must stop the conversation immediately. If things have gone too far the solicitor will have to consider carefully whether (s)he can continue acting for the wife. It is open to the husband to apply to the court, in the interests of justice, for an order barring the wife from relying on her knowledge in this way.

vi) By the same token, if the wife's recollection is that the documents clearly show that the husband is unjustifiably dealing with his assets and that there is therefore a clear risk of dissipation to her prejudice then she can inform her solicitor of this. Subject to the point about privilege mentioned above, the solicitor is entitled to give advice on her recollection and can draft an affidavit in support of a freezing application. But if the wife elects to go down this route she is bound in that affidavit candidly to reveal that her knowledge derives from illegitimately obtained documents,

---

27 *UL v BK (Freezing Orders: Safeguards: Standard Examples)* [2013] EWHC 1735 (Fam).

> and must explain how she got them. She must do this even if this leads to a civil suit or criminal proceedings. That is the price that she will (potentially) have to pay for making an application based on illegitimately obtained knowledge. Of course, there is no question of the wife being forced to incriminate herself as she has a free choice whether to go down this route.'

It is important to note that beach of a spouse's rights to confidentiality could result in a civil claim being issued. The individual could also commit a criminal offence, including pursuant to CMA 1990 or the DPA 2018.

Pursuant to section 1(1) CMA 1990:

(1) A person is guilty of an offence if
- (a) he causes a computer to perform any function with intent to secure access to any program or data held in any computer;
- (b) the access he intends to secure is unauthorised; and
- (c) he knows at the time when he causes the computer to perform the function that that is the case.

Note that the intent a person has to have in order to commit an offence under this section need not be directed at any particular program or data; a program or data of any particular kind; or a program or data held in any particular computer (section 1(2)). A person guilty of an offence under section 1 shall be liable on summary conviction to imprisonment for a term not exceeding 12 months or to a fine not exceeding the statutory maximum or to both; or (c) on conviction on indictment, to imprisonment for a term not exceeding two years or to a fine or to both (section 1(3).

The words of section1(1)(a) should be given their plain and ordinary meaning; an offence under the section does not need to concern the use of one computer to secure access to another; the section is also contravened where an individual causes a computer to perform a function with intent to gain unauthorised access to any program or data held in the same computer.[28] It is unclear whether an offence is committed under section 1 by a person authorised to secure access to computer material, but does so for unauthorised purposes.[29] In *Mangham*,[30] various factors impacting on sentencing were identified in computer hacking cases: planning and persistence; damage to the system itself and to wider public interests, such as national security, individual privacy, public confidence and commercial confidentiality; motive; benefit; revenge (a serious aggravating factor); attempting to sell information wrongly obtained; whether information has been passed onto others; the value of any intellectual property involved; and the offender's psychological profile.[31]

---

28 *Att.-Gen.'s Reference (No. 1 of 1991)* [1993] QB 94, CA.

29 *DPP v Bignell* [1998] 1 Cr. App. R. 1, DC.

30 *R v Mangham* [2012] EWCA Crim 973; [2013] 1 Cr. App. R.(S.) 11.

31 *Archbold Criminal Pleading Evidence and Practice* 2021. Chapter 23 – Criminal Damage and Kindred Offences Part IV. Computer Misuse Act 1990 Section A. Computer Misuse Offences.

These matters should be brought to the client's attention and emphasised in cases where cryptoassets feature.

As with the CMA 1990, clients will also need to be mindful of potential breach of the DPA 2018. Pursuant to section 170 DPA 2018:

> (1) It is an offence for a person knowingly or recklessly—
> (a) to obtain or disclose personal data without the consent of the controller,
> (b) to procure the disclosure of personal data to another person without the consent of the controller, or
> (c) after obtaining personal data, to retain it without the consent of the person who was the controller in relation to the personal data when it was obtained.

The following exceptions, however, apply:

- Obtaining, disclosing, procuring or retaining was necessary to prevent or detect a crime.
- Obtaining, disclosing, procuring or retaining was required or authorised by rule of law or an order of the court or tribunal.
- Obtaining, disclosing, procuring or retaining was in the public interest.
- The defendant acted in reasonable belief that they had a legal right to obtain, disclose, procure, or retain the personal data.
- The defendant acted on the basis that they would have had the consent of the data controller if they had known about the obtaining, disclosing, procuring or retaining and the circumstances of it.
- The defendant acted with a view to the publication by a person of any journalistic, academic, artistic or literary material, and in the reasonable belief that in the particular circumstances, the obtaining, disclosing, procuring or retaining was justified as being in the public interest.
- Obtaining, disclosing, procuring or retaining was necessary to prevent or detect a crime.

The Court of Appeal in *Imerman* considered the earlier legislation, the Data Protection Act 1998. Section 55 of that statute was replicated and enhanced in section 170 DPA 2018. The judgment noted the following:

- There was a 'real possibility that those defendants responsible for accessing Mr Imerman's computer records stored on the server in early 2009 were guilty of an offence under section 1 of the 1990 Act'. Further, that 'There may conceivably be a defence based on the proposition that they believed that they had (or that they actually had) authority to access Mr Imerman's documents stored on server, within the meaning of the Act, because they had, to his knowledge, physically unrestricted access to the server.' [93].

- The defendants also sought to rely on section 35(2) Data Protection Act 2018 which permits disclosure of data if it 'is necessary … for the purpose of, or in connection with, legal proceedings … or is otherwise necessary for the purpose of establishing, exercising or defending legal rights'. Lord Neuberger MR held that 'The issue of necessity lies at the heart of the argument that there is or should be a special dispensation in the Family Division which permits Mrs Imerman to retain copies of documents, prior to the time at which the rules dictate she was entitled to them and without court order. We have resolved that more general but crucial issue against Mrs Imerman (see below). Accordingly, and quite apart from anything else, in so far as it is said to have been "necessary" to protect Mrs Imerman's interests, there is compelling attraction in the argument that it was not necessary, because Mrs Imerman could have applied to the court for a search and seize order or a preservation order rather than her brother, or brothers, taking the law into his, or their, own hands.' [99]

## F. TAXATION

**8.16** Guidance on the taxation of cryptoassets is beyond the scope of this work. However, the following section summarises some of HMRC's current guidance as set out in HMRC's Internal Manual: *Cryptoassets Manual*, which warrants reading in full.[32]

**Specialist advice will need to be obtained as to the tax implications of a party disposing of and/or transferring cryptoassets.**

The manual categorises cryptoassets into exchange tokens, utility tokens, security tokens, and stablecoins. The tax treatment of all types of tokens is dependent on the nature and use of the token and not the definition of the token. HMRC does not consider cryptoassets to be currency or money. This reflects the position previously set out in the Cryptoasset Taskforce report.[33]

The manual is split into different sections for individuals and for businesses.

The manual confirms that in the majority of cases, individuals hold cryptoassets as a personal investment, usually for capital appreciation or to make particular purchases. They will be liable to pay Capital Gains Tax when they dispose of their cryptoassets.[34]

---

32 A copy of the manual is available at: https://www.gov.uk/government/publications/tax-on-cryptoassets. The manual was published on 30 March 2021 and last updated on 22 February 2022.

33 https://www.gov.uk/hmrc-internal-manuals/cryptoassets-manual/crypto10100.

34 https://www.gov.uk/hmrc-internal-manuals/cryptoassets-manual/crypto20050. Further guidance on capital gains tax in this context is contained at https://www.gov.uk/hmrc-internal-manuals/cryptoassets-manual/crypto22000. This section also deals with the tax implications of pooling, fees being satisfied as tokens, blockchain forks, and the effect of losing a private key. Stamp duty, Stamp Duty Reserve Tax, and Stamp Duty Land Tax is addressed here: https://www.gov.uk/hmrc-internal-manuals/cryptoassets-manual/crypto24000.

Individuals will be liable to pay Income Tax and National Insurance contributions on cryptoassets which they receive from: (i) their employer as a form of non-cash payment; and (ii) mining, transaction confirmation or airdrops.[35] The manual notes that there may be cases where the individual is running a business which is carrying on a financial trade in cryptoassets and they will therefore have taxable trading profits. This is likely to be unusual, but in such cases Income Tax rules would take priority over the Capital Gains Tax rules.

Guidance on record keeping in relation to cryptoassets and taxes is contained in a separate part of the manual.[36] This notes that cryptoasset exchanges may only retain transaction records for a short period, while also highlighting the possibility that the exchange may no longer be in existence when an individual completes a tax return. It follows that:

> 'The onus is therefore on the individual to keep their own records for each cryptoasset transaction.
>
> Records of cryptoassets can be:
>
> - paper (cold) wallets containing the individual's public and private keys
> - electronic (hot) wallets on devices
> - other records of their transactions and balances such as downloads of their wallet activity from a cryptoassets exchange
> - hardware (cold) wallets looking like a USB, containing the individual's public and private keys.
>
> Cryptoassets are digital assets and as such all records in a wallet should show balances and transactions, either in full or via reference to a public blockchain. The individual's access to fiat currency could come from:
>
> - the point of deposits into a bank account; and
> - use of a cryptoasset Automated Teller Machine (ATM)
>
> These are records which should also be kept and produced for an enquiry. They form part of the audit trail from acquisition to disposal and therefore evidence of any gains made.
>
> Cryptoasset transactions usually occur on a public blockchain, so can be viewed digitally and checked using records obtained from a wallet. A link to an open source blockchain transaction and acknowledgement of the individual owning the public key involved in the transaction is a record as is a download from their wallet provider or exchange.
>
> Cryptoassets are obtained, administered, exchanged, used and linked to fiat currency electronically or digitally. It is therefore reasonable to request electronic records with full details of transactions and any supporting valuation records for the acquisition and disposal tax points.
>
> Cryptoasset exchanges may only keep records of transactions for a short period, or the exchange may no longer be in existence when an individual completes a tax return.

---

35 https://www.gov.uk/hmrc-internal-manuals/cryptoassets-manual/crypto21000.

36 https://www.gov.uk/hmrc-internal-manuals/cryptoassets-manual/crypto10400.

The onus is therefore on the individual to keep their own records for each cryptoasset transaction, and these must include:

- the type of cryptoasset
- date of the transaction
- if they were bought or sold
- number of units involved
- value of the transaction in pound sterling (as at the date of the transaction)
- cumulative total of the investment units held
- bank statements and wallet addresses, in case these are needed for an enquiry or review.'

Guidance is also provided on the income tax implications of mining (the process by which tokens are awarded for verifying additions to the blockchain). According to HMRC, whether or not this activity amounts to a taxable trade (with the tokens as trade receipts) depends on a range of factors such as: degree of activity, organisation, risk, and commerciality. If the mining activity does not amount to a trade, the pound sterling value (at the time of receipt) of any tokens awarded will be taxable as income (miscellaneous income) with any appropriate expenses reducing the amount chargeable.[37]

Equally, HMRC acknowledges the possibility that in some exceptional circumstances individuals may buy and sell exchange tokens with such frequency, level of organisation and sophistication that the activity amounts to a financial trade in itself:

> 'If the taxpayer's activity is considered to be trading then Income Tax will take priority over Capital Gains Tax and will apply to profits (or losses).
>
> As with any activity, the question whether cryptoasset activities amount to trading depends on a number of factors and the individual circumstances. Whether an individual is engaged in a financial trade through the activity of buying and selling tokens will ultimately be a question of fact. It's often the case that individuals and companies entering into transactions consisting of buying and selling tokens will describe them as 'trades'. However, the use of the term 'trade' in this context is not sufficient to be regarded as a financial trade for tax purposes.
>
> A trade in exchange tokens would be similar in nature to a trade in shares, securities and other financial products. The approach to be taken in determining whether a trade is being conducted or not would also be similar, and guidance can be drawn from the existing case law on trading in shares and securities.'[38]

In terms of valuing cryptoassets for tax purposes, HMRC notes that the value of a gain or loss needs to be converted into pound sterling on the Self-Assessment tax return. If the transaction does not have a pound sterling value (for example if bitcoin is exchanged for Ether) an appropriate exchange rate must be established in order to convert the transaction to pound sterling. According to HMRC, reasonable care should be taken to arrive at an appropriate valuation for

37 https://www.gov.uk/hmrc-internal-manuals/cryptoassets-manual/crypto21150.
38 https://www.gov.uk/hmrc-internal-manuals/cryptoassets-manual/crypto20250.

the transaction using a consistent methodology. Details of the valuation methodology should be retained.[39]

HMRC has also provided guidance on how to determine the location of exchange tokens for tax purposes. As cryptoassets are digital in nature, it follows that they do not have a physical location. However, it is still necessary to determine the *situs* of the asset for tax purposes. According to HMRC, this is particularly relevant for UK resident and non-domiciled individuals when computing their Capital Gains Tax and Inheritance Tax liabilities.[40] The guidance highlights that when considering the *situs* of an asset, the first thing to consider is if there is any statute that specifies the location: 'For CGT purposes, the Taxation of Chargeable Gains Act (TCGA) 1992 provides a number of statutory location rules in sections 275 (location of assets) and 275A (location of certain intangible assets), supplemented by 275B. For IHT purposes there are no statutory rules, determining the location instead relies on general principles applicable to private property.'[41] The guidance then looks at whether there is an underlying asset or no underlying asset as follows:

> '**Underlying Asset**
>
> Section 275 TCGA 1992 provides an exhaustive list of the different types of assets for the purposes of CGT. Where the cryptoasset is simply a digital representation of an underlying asset then the location of the underlying asset will determine the location of the cryptoasset.
>
> **Example**
>
> > ABC Ltd buys and sells gold bullion on behalf of clients. ABC Ltd issues the GoldABC Coin where each token represents the beneficial interest in one gold bar. The GoldABC Coin is a digital representation of a physical asset – the gold bar – and we 'look through' the GoldABC Coin and establish the location of the GoldABC Coin by reference to the underlying asset, being gold bar.
>
> It is possible for a cryptoasset to be a digital representation of another intangible asset, such as share capital or debt, and the relevant rule for determining the location of the underlying asset would determine the location of the cryptoasset.
>
> **No Underlying Asset**
>
> Where the cryptoasset is an asset distinct from any underlying asset then HMRC's view is that none of the statutory rules in the TCGA 1992 apply. Instead it is HMRC's view that:
>
> - exchange tokens have an economic value as they can be 'turned to account' – for example, exchanging them for goods, services, fiat currency or other tokens;
> - exchange tokens are a new type of intangible asset (different to other types of intangible assets, such as shares or debentures); and

39 https://www.gov.uk/hmrc-internal-manuals/cryptoassets-manual/crypto23000.
40 https://www.gov.uk/hmrc-internal-manuals/cryptoassets-manual/crypto22600.
41 Ibid.

- the only identifiable party to consider is the beneficial owner of the exchange token,

  "such that the location of the cryptoasset will be determined by the residency of the beneficial owner"

Using the residency of the beneficial owner of the exchange tokens to determine the location gives a clear, logical, predictable and objective rule which can be easily applied. This means that a person who holds exchanges tokens is liable to pay UK tax if they are a UK resident (as determined by the Statutory Residence Test, see RDRM11000) and carry out a transaction with their tokens which is subject to UK tax.

If an exchange token is co-owned between two or more beneficial owners, then section 275C Taxation of Chargeable Gains Act 1992 applies (for Capital Gains Tax). Each beneficial owner's interest in the asset will be where that beneficial owner is resident. If one or more of the co-owners are UK resident, this will not affect the location for those co-owners who are not UK residents.

For Inheritance Tax, common law is relevant to the extent that Double Taxation Agreements do not determine the location (section 158 of the Inheritance Tax Act 1984).'

# Index

*[all references are to paragraph number]*